RIDE YOUR WAY TO A BOLDER, BRAVER YOU...

Copyright © 2023 Cat Weatherill

The right of Cat Weatherill to be identified as the Author of this Work has been asserted by her in accordance with the Copyright, Designs and Patent Act 1988.

First published in Great Britain in 2023 by Tansy Books

Apart from any use permitted under UK copyright law, this publication may only be reproduced, stores, or transmitted, in any form, or by any means, with prior permission in writing of the publishers or, in the case of reprographic production, in accordance with the terms of licences issued by the Copyright Licensing Agency.

Women's names (True Life Tales) have been changed to protect identities.

Illustrations © Angela Holbrook / MazArty

Cartoons © Anissa Jutami

www.catweatherill.co.uk

CAT WEATHERILL

MOTORCYCLE CONFIDENCE
FOR WOMEN

Illustrated by Angela Holbrook

Tansy Books

CONTENTS

Part 1: Absolute Beginners   15

Part 2: Feeling Alive on a 125   29

Part 3: Clothing   37

Part 4: Building Confidence   47

Part 5: Riding Solo   61

Part 6: Riding With Others   69

Part 7: Parking and Manual Handling   75

Part 8: Whatever the Weather   87

Part 9: Managing Fear and Anxiety   95

Part 10: Dropping the Bike   113

Part 11: Mind Your Language	117
Part 12: Moving Up to a Big Bike	123
Part 13: Preparing for the MODs	131
Part 14: Buying a Big Girl Bike	143
Part15: Life as a Newly Qualified Rider	151
Part 16: Stopping Riding	161
Part 17: Keeping Safe	165
Part 18: Road Tripping Abroad	173
Part 19: Woman in White	182
Resources	185
Milestones	189
Interview with Laura Smith	217

This book was inspired by letters like this...

I did my CBT in early September and have a beautiful little CB125F that I've mainly been practising in local car parks and have ventured out on to the road twice, on my own, for five miles at the most.

I'm having a major crisis of confidence and seriously thinking that maybe I should just stick to being pillion when my partner gets his new bike.

Nothing bad has actually happened to make me lose confidence, am just a serious over thinker and manage to talk myself out of taking the bike out. I stall a fair bit still so try to avoid junctions at all costs!

I worry about holding traffic up while I'm pottering along at 35mph, but really don't feel confident to go any faster. I think maybe I'm my own worst enemy. Has anyone else struggled like this and managed to come out the other side?

Clare x

INTRODUCTION

I was fifty-eight when I started learning to ride a motorcycle.

The instructor wheeled a huge black-and-yellow machine down a ramp, out of the van. I couldn't believe I was planning to actually climb on and attempt to ride.

It was like an enormous wasp. A Honda CB125F.

'What is your dream?' the instructor asked me. 'How far do you plan to take this?'

I had no idea. I honestly hadn't thought that far ahead. An image came into my mind... riding pillion around southern India on the back of a boyfriend's Bullet 500. It was the only bike I could name with any certainty. 'I don't know,' I said. 'Perhaps to ride a Royal Enfield one day?'

Even as I heard myself say that, it seemed such an improbable future event, it wasn't even a proper dream. It wasn't *impossible*. I was there, making a start, after all. But I couldn't imagine it ever happening. I remembered that Bullet 500. To me, it was a beast of a bike. I'd never seen a woman riding one.

To be honest, there was no burning desire to make this thought a reality. Some women have it all mapped out: what they're going to buy, where they're going to go, who they're going to go with. That wasn't me. I was a divorced woman with no friends or family members who rode. Yet something had pulled me in, like the tractor beam in *Star Wars*. I was held in the grip of an inescapable force. I didn't really know what I was saying. I was just going with it.

Looking back now, I see it wasn't about motorcycling really, it was about me. It was about freedom and feeling alive and wanting to expand the horizons of my world. I wanted to feel bigger, stronger, less cautious. *Just do it*, I kept saying to myself. *Just DO IT, woman.*

A motorcycle was literally a vehicle to a braver, bolder me.

So that was why I ended up on a car park in Redditch on a windy Tuesday, looking at a 125 that seemed enormous, saying maybe I would ride an Enfield one day.

That day came just eighteen months later. On holiday in the Canaries, I unexpectedly rode a hired Royal Enfield Interceptor 650. I'd had my full licence for little more than a month.

As I whizzed along the dual carriageway, I realised that not only was I riding on my own, on the other side of the road, with ease and confidence, but I was riding a bigger bike than the one I had named in that improbable dream. And it didn't feel like a beast. In fact, I felt it was a bit under-powered, compared to the 650 I had at home!

So if you are a beginner, struggling with lessons, have faith. You will get there in the end, if you really want to. Your dreams can come true faster than seems possible right now. If I can do it, you can do it too.

Who is this book for?

When I first start writing this book, I thought it would be only for beginners. But it expanded with my own learning journey, which was faster than I ever imagined. I began with my CBT in the summer of 2020. Two years later, I had passed my full licence, ridden 3000 miles across Europe on my beloved 650 and was starting advanced training. It really can happen that fast.

I wanted to write it because I know how it feels to have no one to ask. Some women have partners, family or friends who ride. But what if you don't? What if you *do* know people but feel daft, asking simple questions? What if your partner doesn't understand your anxiety?

In the time it has taken me to write this book, I have found riding partners, and I can say, with full conviction, it is *so* much easier riding with a partner. If you have always ridden with someone, you have no idea how nerve-shredding the simplest of things can be when your are trying to work it out all on your own. Going to a petrol station for the first time is epic. So this book is a big shout-out to all those sisters who are doing it alone, as I did. It might feel like small comfort now, but your sense of achievement will be doubled, believe me.

I especially wanted to write it for anyone who feels anxious. I am no expert. I'm not an instructor. I am a wuss. A real Cautious Kate. That's the truth of it. I had to push through fear, anxiety and self-doubt to achieve my dream of riding a motorcycle. I had days when I cried, days when I nearly gave up, days when I fell off... I thought it would end when I passed my full licence but it didn't. Any rider will tell you, the challenge continues. Fear is ever-present, even for pro racers. They have simply learned how to handle it at the highest level.

Much of the anxiety for beginners is rooted in the fact that they are attempting to do too much, too soon. That is what this book helps with.

I kept a journal throughout my training and noted down things that worked for me. This is what I want to share, in the hope that something will help you.

Dive in where you need to, when you need to. I don't imagine anyone will read the whole book from cover to cover. Our journeys and needs are all so different. You might skip exactly the chapter someone else returns to again and again. That's fine. Take what you want.

It's a very personal view of things. How can it be otherwise? It's based on my experiences, good and bad. I don't offer it as The Right Way of doing things. It's how I did it, no more, no less.

Except for a few tips I've found helpful, I don't offer any technical advice. I leave that to qualified instructors.

I have included some personal stories, because I think sharing such stories helps. At the end of the book there are detailed accounts of my MOD tests. I wasn't planning to include these, I wrote them simply for myself at the time. But I've discovered some learners are keen for first-hand accounts. They really want to know what happens, step-by-step. It helps them imagine how it might be for them.

If you are that kind of learner - enjoy. Those stories are for you. If not, move on!

Some of you more experienced riders might disagree, here and there. Some might feel I making too much of a fuss about it all. Over-thinking things. It's just a bike, for goodness' sake. It's not a fighter jet. Just ride it. What's the problem?

There are some women who go from CBT to full licence in the space of a month. They seem to have no issue with confidence.

This book is not for them. This book is for women like me. Ones who take their time, overthink, fret, blame themselves, whine a bit, wonder what the hell they are doing but keep climbing on the bike to try to get better.

To those sisters, I say: let's do this together!

May your roads be open and smooth and your seat always comfortable.

Cat x

Note: This explains a few terms I've used in the book

CBT is Compulsory Basic Training. This is your first step as a learner. It will be on a 125cc motorcycle.

DAS means Direct Access Scheme. This is the training you do for your full A licence. This will be a 650cc motorcycle. (See **Resources** for more on licences)

Mod 1 is the first part of your DAS test (Module 1)
It takes place on a DVLA test site.

Mod 2 (Module 2) is an on-road test with an examiner following you.

Women's pages I mention these a great deal. They are the pages of female biker groups on Facebook (see **Resources**) I spent a lot of time on these pages during the writing of this book. I didn't want the book to be all me, me, me! I wanted to see what other women were struggling with and how they were fixing it.

My school is the (second) school where I trained - Redditch Motorcycle Training. I am not an instructor! I am still in close contact with RMT, writing blogs and joining advanced training rides. My instructor Laura is interviewed at the end of the book. This is the kind of school I hope you find for your riding journey.

PART 1: ABSOLUTE BEGINNERS

Are you tempted by the idea of motorcycling but are still not sure? Read on…

How does it feel to ride a motorcycle?

There's a famous saying:

Four wheels move the body, two wheels move the soul

Motorcycling is about freedom. The world feels like it's yours. You are free to go wherever you want to go. You can leave all your worries behind.

Biking is very mindful. Some people describe it as meditational. You have to give the road your full attention. You have to stay 'present.' It can be very calming.

It is exhilarating. Nothing compares to that moment when you open up the throttle and the bike responds.

Riding is more sensual than driving. You smell the crops in the fields and the piney scent of a forest as you drive through. You feel the drop in temperature when the sun disappears behind a bank of clouds. You feel the texture of the road and the throb of the engine between your legs. It makes you feel totally alive.

You see the immensity of the sky and the sweep of the ocean. A flock of birds, flying low overhead. The full arc of a rainbow. You feel exposed to the world. Part of it.

You feel proud of your ability to ride. Proud that you made your dream a reality. You feel blessed to have such freedom.

It's tough some days. You might miss the protective cage and comfort of a car. Long rides can be physically exhausting. Wind can cut you to the bone and rain can soak you to the skin. You have to deal with traffic, drivers and difficult road conditions. Your hair can be a mess, your nails mysteriously break inside your gloves and you're bulked up with clothing to the size of a polar bear.

But you know what? It's worth it.

Is it better than riding pillion?

I know many women would say YES! ABSOLUTELY! But I think it depends on how you feel about riding pillion. Personally, I adore riding pillion and feel it has some advantages. There's no pressure, it's warmer and you see far more of the scenery. You can still ride even if you're feeling unwell - a major advantage when touring.

I confess I have found it harder to ride pillion since I learned to ride. I take far more notice of what the rider is doing and it can make me nervous. Riding too close to the car in front, failing to notice things, speeding, making questionable overtakes… I notice it all. My friends are more experienced. They take bends far faster than I can manage. As we hurtle towards one, my whole body will tense up as my brain does the calculation according to *my* riding ability, not theirs!

If you are riding your own bike, you have full control, and this is what many women want. Also on the plus side, the rider's saddle is infinitely more comfortable than the average pillion seat!

'Am I too old to learn?'

At a bike festival, I was amazed to hear a young woman say she had asked herself this question at the age of twenty six.

I started at fifty-eight. A chap at my school recently passed both his Mods at the age of seventy. Motorcycle explorer Steph Jeavons, who runs off-road training sessions in Wales, told me she had an eighty-two year old woman at one of her courses.

I saw a video on YouTube about an American woman who was ninety-six and still riding a Harley Davidson cruiser.

'I like to ride it every week,' she said. 'I'd be on it today, but I couldn't get my leg over this morning!'

Are you too old? No.

Having said this, it might take a little longer if you are older. My brain was definitely sieve-like. I constantly had to write things down, hence the journal I mention so often in this book.

Many of my female biker friends are over fifty, and the usual ageing things come into play: failing eyesight, stiff joints, a tendency to feel very cold. Motorcycling is a physical business. You need to be able to climb onto the bike for starters. That's not something a thirty year-old generally has to consider, but back problems can be challenging in mid-life. Choosing the right bike is essential, long-term.

Creeping anxiety is something many older women struggle with (See **Menopause Matters**)

These things won't stop you. You will learn to do it anyway. Women's groups are great with things like this, either online or in person. I can guarantee someone else will be riding with what is troubling you, from hysterectomy wounds to hip replacements. You will find help and advice.

How long will this journey take?

As long as it needs to. For every woman, it's different.

You can do it in a weekend! You can do your Compulsory Basic Training on the Saturday and be out on the road, on your own, on a 125 motorcycle on the Sunday. You will be displaying L plates, but many riders don't mind that. They love their 125s and don't feel any need to train for a full licence. They simply renew their CBT every two years.

Want a bigger bike? On one of my women's pages recently, a woman went from CBT through Mod 1 to passing MOD 2 in fourteen days. At the other end of the scale, there are women who needed five or six attempts to pass their Mod 1.

It is dependent on so many factors: how well you are trained, how confident you are, how determined you are, how much support you have at home, how much natural ability you have, how much money you can spare… Even the time of year can make a difference.

It is impossible to predict ability. We all learn differently. I thought I would find it fairly easy to step up to a geared bike. I had ridden scooters many times in Asia and already had a CBT certificate when I began my 125 training. But I *really* struggled with the gears and had to go back, week after week. The instructor would give me an hour of car park practice after his CBT students had finished. They had all managed to do it in one day, of course, so I began every session with a crushing sense of incompetence.

Later, when I found a much better school to do my DAS, I was shocked to discover they didn't feel I was ready to move up to a 650, despite having ridden 6000 miles on my 125.

So it can take much longer than you're expecting, and be far more expensive than you were hoping for. Lessons and test days aren't cheap. But you will get there in the end - believe me! If you want it, you will do it.

Why do you want to learn?

Some women are truly shocked when their instructor asks them this question. It can feel too personal, too challenging, too deep. Especially if the next question is *are you doing this for yourself or for someone else?*

'Why' is a really important question. Motivation is your engine. It's what will keeping you going through the down days. And believe me, there *will* be down days, plenty of them, even when you've passed your full licence and have a big bike. It's part of being a biker.

You have to *really* want it. It's going to be tough!

'Where should I learn?'

You will need to find a good training school to do your CBT. If you have biker friends, you might already have a school in mind. If not, join a women's group on Facebook and ask for local recommendations.

Some CBT providers are unscrupulous. I have heard stories of women training on 125s that wouldn't start, were held together with gaffer tape, were missing mirrors… I know money is an issue for many of us, but you don't need this to add to your pressure.

You need a female-friendly school. Sadly, tales of bullying, shouting, sexist language and general intimidation from male instructors are rife. It is deeply unpleasant to experience and can wreck your confidence. The advantage of asking a women's group is that many of the members will be recently trained, so the information will be up to date, and no one is going to recommend a place that made them feel uncomfortable.

Invest in yourself, invest in your future. Ideally you are looking for a school you can go all the way with, from CBT right up to your full licence (if that is your aim.) Believe me, it is a real pain having to re-learn basic techniques because your CBT training was poor. If you need extra DAS training because of it, any saving you made is wiped out.

I am still in regular contact with my school. Since gaining my full licence, I have returned to do several advanced training sessions and am part of their online community. They really do feel like 'family' and that is what you need.

Motorcycling is an ongoing practice, like yoga. There is always more to learn. Find great instructors and you're set for life.

'Help! I have never even sat on a motorcycle…'

Don't worry if you have no experience of motorcycles. Instructors work with complete beginners every day. They start with the absolute basics and help you build the confidence and skills needed for your CBT certificate.

Does it help if you are a driver? Yes and (possibly) no. Yes because it means you have more road experience and are likely to see hazards faster. Possibly no because you will bring your driving style with you and it might not be helpful. As a driver, for example, I can be very casual at junctions, waiting for cars to pass when I could easily have gone. As a rider, all my trainers have urged me to be far more assertive.

Does it help if you can ride a bicycle? Yes! Many off-road schools put their students onto bicycles to help develop their balance. If you struggle with slow manoeuvres - the U turn, the figure of eight - practising on a car park on a bicycle can really help.

'Will I need biking clothes to do my CBT?'

Most schools will provide the basics if you don't have them: helmet, gloves and jacket. You will need to wear thick denim jeans and sturdy boots (like Doc Martens) These will need upgrading later if you start riding your own bike.

It's also a good idea to take your own headphones, especially if you struggle to get a comfortable fit. The instructor will be talking to you through a wireless connection ('comms') when you are out on the road.

'Will I need to prepare anything?'

You should read the Highway Code if you are new to the road and re-read it if you are a driver. This sounds like a chore, but it really isn't. The Highway Code is designed to protect and help you. Knowing what is legal (and what is not) will save you from getting points on your licence.

What will happen on the day

CBT training begins on a car park. You will be introduced to the controls of the bike then learn how to pull away and stop safely and under control. Then you'll practise riding, doing large figures of eight, learning clutch control, using the gears etc. There should be a 'classroom' element when you discuss hazards and road signs. Finally, when you are road ready, there should be a two-three hour ride out on public roads with the instructor.

After a de-briefing, you will get your certificate, if the instructor feels you have reached the required standard: you are not a danger to yourself or other road users.

The whole day should take around six hours. If the school is saying it will be significantly shorter, find another school.

'Help! I didn't get my CBT...'

If you reach the end of the day and the instructor feels you're not quite there, they will ask you to return for a bit more practise. This is common but can still be gut-wrenching if you had it in your head it would all be done in one day.

It does NOT mean:

- You have failed.

- You will never be able to do it.

- You will never be able to ride a big bike because you clearly don't have what it takes.

- You have done badly that day.

- You are a loser / useless / whatever else you like to beat yourself down with.

CBT isn't a test. It is a standard to be reached. Once you have reached the required level, they *will* issue the certificate. So it's simply a question of time. Persevere. If you want it, you will get it.

Learning to ride is hard. There's a huge amount of information to take on board. Feeling overwhelmed is very common!

Dropping the bike is also common on a CBT ('dropping' a bike is when it falls to the ground because the balance has gone beyond the point where you can hold it upright.) Falling off the bike happens too, along with hitting kerbs, going into hedges and bursting into tears. Bruises are frequent. Broken bones are not common but I have read posts from women who broke wrists and ankles. So if you had a bad day, you are one of a gang!

How good is your teacher?

'If you are struggling, it's my fault. I haven't taught you well enough. I haven't explained it in a way you could understand.'

Mr Harding, my maths teacher at school

Did you have a teacher at school who really inspired you? Someone you can still remember after ten, twenty, thirty or more years?

I can still remember Mr Harding telling me this. It transformed my thinking. I wasn't stupid or useless. I simply needed it to be explained differently.

We all learn in different ways and a good teacher will be able to adapt to suit you. Unfortunately, some instructors adopt a one-size-fits-all approach to their training. This is lazy and unhelpful, because if it's a bad fit for you, it will slow you down. It's like trying to walk in a pair of shoes that are too big for you.

If you find anything about your learning relationship negative, think very seriously before committing to any further training with this instructor. You can waste a lot of time and money trying to make those bad shoes fit. You do not have to settle for the first instructor you find. There will always be other options.

True Life Tales: Mona's Story

Mona was looking for reassurance online as she faced her fourth attempt at getting her CBT.

Four times? That didn't sound right to me. We began to chat, privately. She said she felt very alone, awkward and her anxiety was getting worse.

I said that if she didn't get her CBT this time, she should look for a different school.

'Oh no, my instructors are really good,' she said. 'It's just me.'

I told her about my early training as I struggled to transition from a scooter to a geared bike. After four hours on the 125 (which I had already dropped) the instructor lost his patience and declared we were going out on the road, whether I was ready or not.

'What else are you going to do?' he said. 'Ride round and round a car park for the rest of your life?'

So we went out on the road, where I promptly hit a kerb and came off.

I went home in tears. Why was I doing something that was giving me no pleasure whatsoever? Was motorcycling so important that I was prepared to die for it? That's where I felt it was heading.

I came *so* close to giving up. The only thing that stopped me was the fact that I had a CBT, gained on a scooter. So I decided I would buy a 125, exactly the same model as the one I had been learning on, and I would practise on my own. And that was what I did.

'But the point I am making is *this*,' I wrote to Mona. 'At no stage did I blame the instructor. How could it be his fault? He was ex-police. He had been riding for forty years. He was great company when he wasn't bullying me. He seemed very kind. No, it was always *me*. I was the useless one.'

'I do that too!' she replied. 'Internalise everything. Go round and round in spirals.'

'And this training school,' I said, 'do they charge you for every extra day?'

'Yes…'

(I am pleased to say that Mona was given her CBT certificate on her fourth attempt and is now the proud owner of a 125)

Did you know…?

Some training schools offer a two-day CBT course, enabling you to learn with a lot less pressure. You also leave with a stronger skill set, giving you a firmer foundation to build upon. I really wish I had taken this route!

The Scooter Route

A scooter (sometimes referred to as a 'twist and go') is easier to ride than a motorbike because it doesn't have gears. Speed is controlled by your right hand turning the throttle (the accelerator) There are also two brake levers, just like a pedal bike: one for the front brake and one for the back.

This is the easiest way to get a CBT and, surprisingly, it allows you legally to ride a geared 125 bike too. So if you are *very* anxious, this can be a way in. You get your CBT out of the way on a scooter (in one day) and then start learning to ride a geared bike with far less pressure.

The disadvantage of this route is that you learn to use your left hand for the back brake. So when you step up to a geared bike, your brain has to remember your left hand is now your clutch and the back brake has moved to your foot!

I also found scooter riding made me a bit rough and 'grabby' with the brakes when gentle pressure is what is needed on a geared bike. It took a lot of undoing and re-learning to break this habit, but to be fair, I had ridden a lot of scooters.

Be wary of schools that push you towards doing your CBT on a scooter when you really want to do it on a geared bike. They are saying it for *their* benefit, not yours. They simply want to get you through fast and take your money.

They might say you're too short to ride a bike or suggest it's easier for a woman to learn on a scooter. This is nonsense. If you are short, you simply need a lowered bike.

What is a 'lowered' bike?

A lowered bike is a bike that has had its saddle lowered, making it easier for shorter riders to put their feet on the ground. Everything else stays the same.

A good training school will have lowered bikes, both 125s and 650s.

What is a 'pre-CBT'?

This is something you don't need to do, legally speaking, but it's getting increasingly common. Call me cynical, but it seems a perfect way for unscrupulous schools to cash-in on the rising number of women riders. Already I have read posts by women who have been pressured to pay for it.

If they sense you are a raw, anxious beginner, they might suggest you do a two or three-hour 'pre-CBT' as a way of calming your nerves and getting familiar with the bike. They will suggest that on your CBT day, you might be with others who are more experienced than you are.

This might indeed be true. I did a CBT lesson with two guys in their twenties who had been riding trail bikes for ten years. They were doing CBT simply because they wanted to move onto road bikes. They needed the piece of paper. They definitely did not have to learn how the throttle worked!

But still, this is not a reason to do a pre-CBT. The whole point of a CBT is learning the basics of riding a motorcycle, even if you have never been on one before. When you were learning to drive a car, did you do pre-driving lessons?

Pre-CBTs play on anxiety, right from the start. I don't like that. They plant the idea that you are facing something so challenging, you'll never manage it 'cold' in a day. That is simply not true.

If you are very raw or nervous, instead of 'pre-CBT,' look for a school that offers a 'Taster Session.' This will be shorter (sixty - ninety minutes) and cheaper. To me, a Taster is much more positive-looking. It gives you an opportunity to familiarise yourself with the bike and see how you feel about it before committing to a CBT. You have the luxury of wobbling around a car park with no one watching!

A Taster also gives you a 'taste' of the school and the instructor. How did they make you feel? Confident or intimidated? It is so important to find someone who inspires confidence.

'Help! I did my CBT and didn't enjoy it...'

Motorcycling is not for everyone. Sometimes it is very easy to get swept along by a dream. Reality can turn out to be very different.

Some women are shocked at how scary it is once they are taken out of the car park and onto the road. It feels *very* different to being in a car, with its airbags, seat belts and cocoon of metal. You feel totally vulnerable - and you *are* vulnerable. You will soon learn that many drivers don't give a damn that you are on a motorcycle, trying to do your best. That you have L plates. That you are female. In fact, for some drivers, this just seems to add to their spite.

Overwhelmingly, women riders will tell you it's only a matter of confidence, that you have to get out there on the road and start learning. I agree with that. As someone who so nearly gave up, I can tell you that for me, getting out on the road on my own 125 was the way to push through. So maybe that is what you need to do too? I would encourage you to give it a proper go before throwing in the towel. No, more than that - I would *urge* you to reconsider and give it another chance, because already you have passed the first hurdle. You are not a raw beginner anymore - you have gained a little experience to carry forward.

Having said this, learning to ride a motorcycle is like starting a romantic relationship. Some women will fall madly in love and their passion will last a lifetime. Some will have a joyous love affair for a few years then decide it's time to move on. Some will end it after a few dates; they know in their heart, it wasn't right for them.

Motorcycling is supposed to be pleasurable - right?

PART 2: FEELING ALIVE ON A 125

'Should I buy a 125?'

Yippee! You have your CBT! You've drunk the prosecco and eaten the cake. What next?

You can now legally ride a 125 on the road, alone, displaying L plates. For many people, this is more than enough. A 125 is fine for their needs and they're not bothered by the L plates. A 125 is only as limiting as you allow it to be. I chatted online with a woman who was planning to get a full licence so she could take her 125 to France.

'I'm a cyclist,' she told me. 'I go to Normandy all the time on my road bike, doing the back lanes, so I know what it's like. I don't need anything bigger.'

A 125 is a proper motorbike, it's not a toy. Some can do 70 mph. They are cheap and reliable and make perfect commuter bikes.

So should you buy one?

Some women will move straight onto DAS training within days of getting their CBT, so for them buying a 125 would be a definite no. But for me, it was always a yes. At that time, handling a 125 was challenge enough for me. I wasn't convinced I would *ever* want to move up.

Some people say it's a waste of money, buying a 125 if you plan to move up, but there's something to be said for taking your time and enjoying the journey. If you move straight onto a big bike, you miss out on the fun of owning a 125 - and they can be *enormous* fun! I took mine to places where I won't go on my 650. She was much lighter, much easier to park and I had less fear of dropping her.

I had my 125 (a Honda CB125F) for a little over a year, from July 2020 to September 2021. I didn't ride from October to late March. Not only was it cold, but the thought of riding on ice was frankly terrifying. So I had about eight months of actual use and rode over six thousand miles on her.

Gorgeous summer rides around the Cotswolds, stopping to photograph cottages and eat cake in village tea rooms… I went off on spontaneous adventures. One day I saw a post on Facebook about a cafe on a narrow boat, travelling round the canals in the Midlands. They gave their location for that day. Within the hour, I was riding in search of them. Soon I was drinking coffee on a stunning stretch of canal, miles from anywhere, surrounded by rolling hills with a bowl of sapphire sky above.

I didn't have to go far to feel alive. Very often (almost daily!) I would decide to go for a ride in the evening, heading out around six o'clock. The roads would be quietening and it always blew away the fatigue of the day.

Having a 125 really builds your confidence. I went into my DAS with hours of road experience under my belt. As my Mod 2 approached, I spent my evenings riding around all the known test routes in my area. I knew which roads had rough surfaces, how sharp some innocent-looking bends were, how steep the side roads could be. I knew it so well, I had no surprises on my test. That was all because of the hours I spent on my 125.

I also loved posting up my photos on social media. I felt like I'd found a new version of me and I really liked her.

So I would say buy a 125 and enjoy every minute of her. Would I buy an expensive one? No, there's no real need. There are plenty of cheap ones in good condition and, if you are planning to move up to a full licence, you will be selling her. I was happy to have one with a few scratches and I never once washed her!

Having said this, I am on a budget. If you have unlimited funds, go ahead and buy whatever you want! That's enjoying the journey, isn't it?

'Help! I am worried about what others think of me...'

This is a real biggie for many women. Often it is the first hurdle to overcome. You can be so worried, you won't even have the confidence to book a CBT, however much you dream of riding.

You're not alone. No one likes the thought of wobbling round like a six year-old in front of others. But it has to be done. There's no other way of getting to where you want to be.

Here are a few things that might help.

Firstly, who are these 'others' you are worried about? If they are complete strangers - who cares about them? Imagine you are watching someone struggle to park their car. Your head might be full of thoughts about them in that moment. But once the car is parked, do you still carry those thoughts? No. Your attention moves on because it's of no real consequence to you. You don't care, to put it bluntly. It's the same with strangers watching you. Any thoughts they have will dissipate like smoke as soon as you've gone.

If they are other bikers, they will (or should) understand. They've been there too!

If the 'others' are friends or family, it can be difficult. Hopefully they will be supportive and encouraging. Proud of what you are achieving, because you are doing something *really* special here, following your dream. It matters to you and it's not easy. You'll need all the help you can get and they need to understand and respect that. If they don't, your journey will be harder. So dig deep, draw strength and have the conversation.

Work only with known facts

Unless people tell you explicitly what they are thinking, you do not know what's in their head. You are guessing and you might be wrong. Remember that person struggling to park their car? Not everyone watching will be thinking unkindly. Some will be thinking 'Dear Lord, I'd be struggling too, with a space that small' or 'She's determined to get in there. Good for her! I'd have given up by now.'

You can't stop people thinking, but don't assume it's all bad. Women riders are still something of a novelty. Many people will be thinking good thoughts about you. You're having a go, doing your best, making progress, learning new skills, practising what you've learned so far... These are all praise-worthy things. If someone thinks (or says) otherwise, it says everything about *them* and nothing about *you*.

Let it go

There's a wonderful Buddhist story about two monks, one old and one young, who reach a river crossing where they find a curvaceous young woman who wants help getting across.

The older monk graciously offers to carry her over. To the younger monk's horror, the young woman hitches her skirt up over her thighs and the old monk carries her piggy-back across the river. Once on the far side, he puts her down and they go their separate ways.

The monks walk on for some miles but the young monk is silently fuming. At last he can bear it no longer.

'What were you *thinking?*' he says. 'Carrying her like that? Have you no shame?'

The older monk smiles. 'Yes, I carried her,' he says, 'but I left her back there on the riverbank. You, my young friend, are carrying her still.'

Whatever happens, let it go and move on.

Take Control

What exactly are you worried people are thinking? Is it something along the lines of 'she's a rubbish rider,' 'she can't handle that bike' or 'she shouldn't be on the road?'

These are all rooted in the fear of being incompetent. You can do something about this - get better! Whatever it is, practise, practise, practise. Find a good car park and put in the hours. Whether it's being unable to manually handle your bike or wobbling on u-turns, practise is always the answer.

Sometimes there is a grain of truth in what we believe others are thinking about us. We are giving voice to our own unconscious thoughts. Imagine you're serving your guests a homemade apple pie. If you feel confident in your ability to cook apple pie, you'll serve it up without a worry. But if you know your pastry is sometimes a bit dry or you don't always add enough sugar, you might worry about their judgement. Biking is the same!

Take control of your competence. There's no need to be a victim here.

Top Box Worries

I love my top box. It means I don't have to carry my helmet with me when I stop to have a coffee and wander.

You're unlikely to notice any difference if you add a top-box to your bike. They don't unbalance you.

They sit on a plate that needs to be attached to the bike. The box can be removed with a simple 'push' action once the box is open.

Removing the box can be a good idea on a windy day - it reduces the buffeting. Alternatively you can eat a bigger slice of cake during your cafe stop to add extra ballast to your backside!

When Your Bike Won't Start

Motorcycles have something called a 'kill switch.' It's a way of instantly stopping the engine in an emergency. Unfortunately, it's very easy to switch on by accident and, if it is in the 'on' position, your bike won't start. Many a seasoned rider has been flummoxed by this one!

So if your bike won't start, check the kill switch first before thinking 'battery' or something else.

This tip is especially for those learning alone. It can be very hard having no one to ask. You can feel a right donut. Women's pages are useful for solving problems like this. I remember one woman who had just bought a 125 and was completely baffled by one of the keys on the key ring. She had looked all over the bike but couldn't find a hole to fit it.

It turned out to be the key for a Givi top box (which the bike no longer had) It might sound a trivial matter, but I could absolutely understand her bewilderment. Also her anxiety. Was there something that needed to be turned on for the bike to work properly?

If you ever find yourself thinking 'Is this just me?' the answer is NO!

Incidentally, leaving your bike with the kill switch on can be a useful anti-theft trick. Opportunist thieves have it in their heads to get on and go. If they find the bike *won't* go, it can throw them. Crazy but true!

The 125 Revolution

Sales of 125 are rocketing, especially in urban areas. The uber-cool Birmingham manufacturer Mutt *only* makes 125s. Mutt bikes are gorgeous, retro-styled machines and they cannot produce them fast enough. There is a waiting list for them at their new London store (muttmotorcycles.com)

 Lexmoto (lexmoto.co.uk) specialise in 125s. Check out the Sinnis Hoodlum 125 too (sinnismotorcycles.com)

Whether you want a cruiser, a retro roadster, a sports bike or a naked classic, you will find a 125 version you can be proud of.

Many women adore their Honda Groms and wouldn't ride anything else. My riding buddy Jon loves his Honda Monkey, another 125cc machine. His mates have bought Monkeys too, and they go away for weekends. These are guys in their fifties who have been riding for thirty-plus years and own big bikes. But they leave them at home and take the Monkeys instead. Last year, Jon did twice as many miles on his Monkey as he did on his Triumph Speed Twin.

He keeps telling me: 'You must have a go. Once you try it, you'll want one.'

I believe him!

'Help! It is taking me far longer to learn than everybody else...'

Here's how it goes. You've been going out on your 125 but you still feel very much a learner. You've joined a few online women's groups but keep seeing posts from other learners who make it sound easy. No sooner have they done their CBT, they're onto Mod 1 and asking for big bike options, while you are still trying to complete a ride without accidentally going into neutral half a dozen times (surely I wasn't the only one to do that?!)

It's easy to start doubting your ability. It's taking you *so* much longer...

The truth is, you can't compare yourself to other learners because you don't know their journey. Many women have been around bikes since childhood and, as we all know, having positive role models can really boost self-confidence. Some women have ridden off-road since their teens. Some have had car park lessons from their partners before their CBT. Whereas for you, that CBT day might have been the first time you'd ever sat on a bike.

Keep faith, keep a journal and keep going. You've got this!

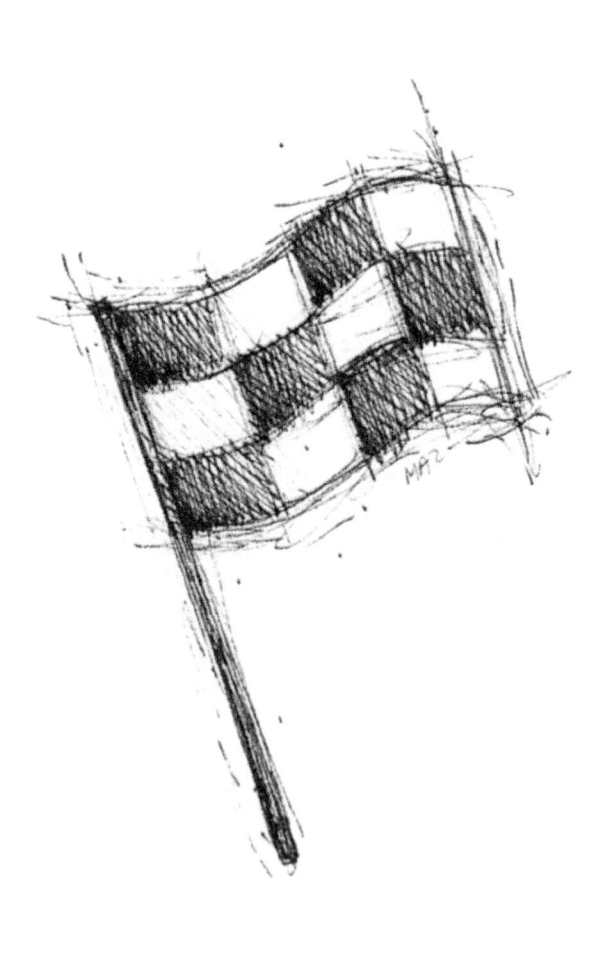

PART 3: CLOTHING

Once you've passed your CBT, you will need to think of getting some proper biking gear if you want to stay safe and comfortable. There are three things you will soon discover:

1 Protective gear is expensive

2 You will need more than one set, because of the weather

3 Sizing can be a nightmare!

Where do I begin?

Ideally, go to a store where you can try things on. I went to a branch of Sports Bike Shop and was there for three hours, buying my first basic kit of a jacket, helmet, boots, jeans and gloves. The staff were extremely helpful, especially with the helmets. The one I had picked out online turned out to be an appalling fit, completely wrong for the shape of my head. It was brilliant having someone to guide me.

With Sports Bike Shop, you can order items online before visiting. It doesn't cost anything and it means you won't get there only to find they don't have your size. They are a bit like Argos, with huge back rooms full of stock, but they can't keep everything, especially in the smaller stores.

Safety Codes: what to look for

You will find endless trousers and jackets online, but not all of them will offer true protection.

Clothing is rated from AAA (the highest eg racing leathers) to C.

Jackets and jeans should have pockets inside them to hold 'protectors.' This is the armouring. You should look for CE Certified protectors. These come in two levels, 1 and 2. Level 2 offers higher protection than level 1.

You need to be aware that cheap clothing might boast about CE ratings when the actual garment might not have any protection level at all. They are talking about the *protectors* used, not the fabric. Some very cheap imports do not even offer CE rated protectors.

The hugely popular MotoGirl company spends thousands of pounds ensuring their clothes meet the highest safety standards. Read this for a full explanation of ratings: https://motogirl.co.uk/pages/ce-certification

Reputable dealers like Sports Bike Shop only stock clothing that meets the required standards.

Jackets

A jacket is essential. I bought a textile jacket with a removable inner lining and still wear it now, from April/May to October. But even with the lining removed, it is too warm for hot days, so I later bought a summer jacket. It's not warm enough for truly cold days, even with multiple layers beneath, so I bought a winter-weight one. Every biker understands this need for more, more and more!

When trying on a jacket, sit down and lean forward, like you are on your bike. Don't worry about looking daft - everyone does this. Or should! It's really important. You are looking for gaps where the wind can get in.

Do the sleeves ride up, exposing your wrists?

Does it ride up at the back, leaving a gap between the jacket and your trousers?

If the answer is yes, don't buy it. You will regret it later.

'What size should I buy?'

Until you ride, you have no idea how cold it can get. I had ridden pillion and been cold, sitting there for hours on end. But it's nothing compared to the battering the rider takes. The wind cuts you to the bone, and I find it can do that even on apparently mild days.

For your first jacket, I would recommend leaving room for several layers underneath it. With my textile jacket, I often wear a base layer, tee shirt and sweater plus the inner lining. So don't buy anything too snug. You can take these layers with you and put them on in the shop to get a good fit.

This makes sense when you're only going to have one jacket. It might look bulkier than you would like, but you can find more flattering shapes later. What you need, when you're starting out, is one that will cover most bases.

Trousers

There's a huge range here. Again, you will find that you need different weights for different seasons. But to get you going (assuming you are riding from May - October) Kevlar jeans can be a good choice. That was what I started with, and they got me through my first season.

What is Kevlar?

Kevlar was first used in the 1970s as a replacement for steel in racing tyres. It is so strong (five times stronger than steel) it's used in bulletproof vests and army combat helmets. It can also be woven into fabric, making the fabric far more resistant to abrasion and heat.

Basically, if you come off your bike and slide across the tarmac, Kevlar clothing buys time for your skin. We are talking seconds here, but every second counts. The skin can be completely torn off if you slide for long enough. Kevlar jeans take longer to shred than regular jeans.

What are jeggings?

Jeggings are a cross between leggings and jeans. They generally offer less protection than jeans but they are more comfortable, especially in the warmer weather. They are a tighter fit than jeans, but this doesn't necessarily mean they are more flattering! Some can be very wrinkly. You really need to try them.

With both jeans and jeggings, look for a high waist. Jeggings especially can be cut too low at the back, especially if you ride a racer. Try them on sitting down and sitting forward, like you would on your bike.

What are mesh trousers?

Mesh trousers look like regular textile trousers until you hold them up to the light. Then you will see they are perforated like a tea bag. This means the air circulates much more freely, cooling you down.

They are perfect for summer riding if you find other options are making you too sweaty. I would not have coped on my European trip without mesh trousers: the temperature was 35 - 40 degrees every day. Even with mesh, I was baking when the traffic was slow-moving.

The only downside with them is they can feel cold extremely quickly if the weather changes, even if it's something as simple as a sunny day turning cloudy or windy. They offer no protection in that sense. But in heatwaves, they are a godsend.

They have armouring at the knees and hips, just like regular textile trousers. Mesh jackets are available too.

'Can I wear ordinary jeans?'

Legally, yes. But they have no resistance to abrasion. If you come off the bike, they will not protect your skin as you slide across the tarmac.

Leathers

I have never worn leathers (a one-piece suit with a zip up the front) so I asked a group of my women friends for comments. To my amazement, no one had anything good to say! Everyone preferred textiles for general riding.

'They're cold when it's cold, hot when it's hot and wet when it's wet' was one reply.

'They're hellish when you need the loo!' was another.

So why are leathers so popular?

Pro racers will tell you: nothing protects you better than leather. It is extremely good at resisting abrasion. It can also be extremely comfortable - the best leather is strong but supple. It moulds to the shape of your body with time.

This (according to my friends) is why it is difficult to get good second-hand leathers. They will be moulded to the shape of the previous owner and will not easily re-shape to fit you. If you buy them new, they can take a long time to break in. They are also designed to be form-fitting, so if it gets cold, you might not have room for layers underneath.

None of this will put you off buying them if you want them! Leathers are potent, for sure. If you fancy them, the general advice seems to be you get what you pay for. Cheap imports won't offer the same protection as quality leathers. Ready-made will always be a compromise on fit; handmade is more comfortable.

You can get leather separates, of course. Many instructors wear leather trousers, as do the police, which makes me wonder about that 'cold and wet' comment.

I bought a secondhand leather jacket online and love it. It feels very different to my textile jackets. It seems to do a better job of keeping out the wind and it's warmer - I often don't need the sweater layer. Because I'm not so bulked-up, it always feels easier to manoeuvre the bike.

Gloves

Gloves are one of the hardest things to fit, especially if you have small hands. Usually the fingers are too long, giving you a spare couple of centimetres at the tip. Who wants that, when you're trying to get a neat grip on the levers?

They can be wide in the palm, too short at the wrist… It is best if you can go to a shop and try them on, because they are not cheap. You will find plenty for sale online though, barely worn. People are very quick to get rid of badly-fitting gloves because they are so important. If they are wrong, they can affect your whole ride.

You will need two pairs, one for summer and one for colder weather. If you are doing DAS, make sure you buy your gloves early and get them broken-in.

Winter gloves can take a *very* long time to break in. Whenever I start wearing mine after the summer, I hear myself over-revving the bike. It's like riding wearing oven mitts, no feeling whatsoever.

Boots

Boots come in various styles, from classic biker boots to ones that look more like racing boots. If you are on the shorter side, you can get boots with built-up heels and soles. This will make it easier to flat foot (put your foot down flat when you are stopped) Look for Daytona boots.

Many beginners like trainer-style boots because they are softer to wear. They have ankle protection and have the bonus of looking just like normal trainers - perfect if you're heading to a cafe to meet non-biker friends.

Be warned that boots can take a long time to wear in and feel familiar. If you are planning to wear them for a test, make sure you buy them well in advance. I was shocked when I bought my first pair of proper biking boots: I was constantly hitting neutral or the gear wouldn't shift. It took several rides before I had the feel of them.

Many women recommend wearing new boots around the house to break them in. Saddle soap can soften very hard leather.

You will need proper boots to do DAS. For a CBT, most schools say 'sturdy boots' like Doc Martens will suffice. Definitely not trainers.

'Can I wear Doc Martens permanently?'

You can wear whatever you want, to be truthful. Millions of journeys are made every year by people in flip flops. But if you come off the bike, flip flops will offer no protection to your feet, nor will trainers.

Motorcycle boots have specially reinforced soles plus armouring for the ankle and heel. Doc Martens, while sturdy, don't have this and the leather and stitching might not hold up in a slide across the tarmac.

As for work boots, I was once told to avoid steel toe caps because in a crash, they can amputate your toes, but this might be a myth!

Helmets

Beware of cheap online helmets. They don't always meet the minimum safety standard.

Also be careful at bike shows. Trading standards officers find sub-standard helmets even at prestigious events, so clearly anyone can hire a stall. I've heard of people buying boxed helmets only to discover there's a problem when they get home. And who is going to pay for a second day's event ticket, just to return something?

Used helmets might have been dropped, even if they look perfect.

Value your life. Buy from a respectable dealer. They will offer a fitting service too.

I bought my first helmet from Sports Bike Shop and was so glad I did. I had picked out one online that looked good, but when I tried it on in the shop, it was a terrible fit. A very helpful assistant told me it was completely the wrong shape for my head and steered me in the direction of others. He showed me really useful things, like how to know when a helmet is too big for you. He also suggested I buy a *pin lock*, which I had never heard of. It's a kind of mini-visor that is fixed to the inside of your visor to stop it fogging up. Brilliant!

They fitted it in the shop for me for me - for free, I think? If not, it was only a couple of pounds extra and well worth it.

Make sure your helmet has a built-in sun visor. It won't cost much more and makes your life *so* much easier. Wearing sunglasses inside your helmet can be a real pain and once they're on, they're on. With a built-in sun visor, you can slide it up and down when needed. This is great on a cloudy day and can literally prove a lifesaver if you suddenly find yourself heading into a long, dark road tunnel.

Neck Tubes

A neck tube is a loop of thin fabric that you wear instead of a scarf to keep your neck warm. They make a huge difference in colder weather because you can pull them up like a hood and put your helmet on top.

You can also pull them up to help keep headphones in place. They stop your hair being blown by the wind too.

Hair Care

Some women report no problems with their hair. For others, it's a nightmare.

The last time I went to my hairdresser, she said to me, 'It's just breaking off.' My hair used to be way past my shoulders. Now it is barely touching them. Nothing has changed in my hair routine except I started riding. It can only be wind damage.

Even if you don't get breakage, you can get tangles or arrive looking a complete mess.

Some women plait their hair. Some use thin neck tubes, pulled up. Some use satin sleep cap or scrub caps, like medics wear.

There is another option I have yet to try. It's called Hightail and it's a pouch that attaches to the back of your helmet. You slip your hair inside.

It is expensive, but women who use it swear it's a game-changer. I'm going to give it a go!

See **Resources** for links.

Winter Riding

If you are planning to ride all year round, you will need to look at serious waterproofs and heated clothing. Heated items include gloves, socks, jackets, waistcoats, trousers and inner soles for your boots. Heated handgrips for the bike are great too.

PART 4: BUILDING CONFIDENCE

True Life Tales: Sal's Story

Sal was posting on a women's page because she had returned home from a ride feeling terrified.

She wrote:

I passed my CBT last week. Today I went out on my 125 for the first time, with my hubby and came home terrified, feeling like I'm going to kill myself out there. Couldn't corner! Went right over the middle line twice. Thank God there was nothing coming the other way. Advice please??

Replies started flooding in, all very kind and supportive. Everyone wanted to help. But some of the advice given was way too advanced for a learner. It was just more information to process when Sal was struggling even to apply what she'd already learned.

Learning to ride a motorcycle isn't easy. Your brain has to work extremely hard to juggle a host of unfamiliar elements: how to change gear, how to speed up, how to slow down, how to stay balanced on a machine that is moving through space faster than a human being is designed to go. Then you add in observation skills, judging the speed and distance of oncoming vehicles, calculating the angle of turns, anticipating what other vehicles will do, reacting to unexpected developments...

No wonder Sal was feeling overwhelmed. She was trying to do too much, too soon.

Sal had gone out with her hubby just a few days after passing her CBT. It was the first time she had ridden her 125. Her hubby was being kind and supportive, taking her for a ride

She had done her CBT, so she had been out on the road with an instructor for a couple of hours. She could ride, couldn't she? No problem.

Except there *was* a problem. Sal found it beyond her skill level and came home traumatised as a result.

To be fair, not every woman has this kind of experience, first time out. There are plenty of posts that say:

Today I went out on my 125 for the first time with my hubby and LOVED EVERY MINUTE!!!

Everyone is different. Some women have bags of confidence, no fear and find it comparatively easy to handle a bike, even as a beginner.

I was not one of those women. The first time I went out on my 125, I was so wary, I only turned left.

I am not alone in this! I know other women instinctively did exactly the same thing.

I got up at 6 am so no one would see me pushing the bike out of its parking space. I went alone. I had my route planned. I went round in a loop, going left at every junction.

I went round this loop several times, then did a slightly longer loop, still turning only left. I looped for an hour then went home and was parked up before the morning traffic began.

The next day, I began by doing the left-turning loop then went around one of the roundabouts and did it in reverse. Now it was all right turns!

Dear readers, by now I am guessing you have split into two camps. There are those who are thinking: *Seriously? This was all she was capable of?*

And others who are thinking: *Oh my God. This is genius.*

All I can say is this: it worked for me. Every day my confidence grew. By the end of a week, I was ready to tackle the local dual carriageway - in the afternoon! I rode to a retail park in a bigger town, handling the busier roads and the car park. I felt like a real champion. Unlike Sal, I never came home terrified, feeling I was going to get myself killed. I felt very safe, was totally loving it and felt enormously proud of myself. *I could do this.*

If you are like I was - keen to learn but lacking confidence - here's how I did it, step by step -

Small Steps Training Plan

For me, route planning was the key to building confidence. I could ride out, on my own, confident I wouldn't have to face anything beyond my ability.

The second key element was my journal (see below)

When you are comfortable with a stage, move on to the next.

1. To prepare for your very first ride out on your 125, plan your route the night before: a small loop and a bigger loop around your neighbourhood, doing only LEFT turns.

2. Go round the loops several times.

3. Do the same route in reverse, giving you RIGHT turns only.

4. Plan and ride a route that gives you lefts and rights.

5. Plan and ride a route that brings in new elements eg a stretch of dual carriageway.

6. Set a destination with a reward built in. A trip to a retail park is perfect for this. Plan your route in advance. Think about it, step by step. Will you need to change lanes at any time? Be clear in your head. If you're feeling anxious, do it by car first. Get familiar with the route - familiarity brings comfort. Ride there, have a coffee, buy something small and ride home. Celebrate your achievement. Be proud!

7. Start exploring your local neighbourhood. Begin by planning your routes then move on to unfamiliar roads. This will throw up some unexpected moments - a junction that seems easy in a car can be unexpectedly steep on a bike. But you *will* handle it and your confidence will get a massive boost!

8. Set a goal. Choose a location that is a thirty minute ride away. As before, study the route and plan in advance. Try to include a challenging element. (I chose a town that had a 10% hill on the way in and out) A visit to a friend can be good for this.

9. Set a goal that is further away. Now you are flying!

'JUST TAKE IT STEP BY STEP.
START SMALL.
ENJOY THE PROCESS OF BEING BETTER THAN YOU WERE THE DAY BEFORE.
PRETTY SOON YOU'LL BE WHERE YOU NEVER IMAGINED YOU COULD BE'

Jessica Zahra, long distance adventure rider

'When should I start riding with others?'

When you feel happy to would be my answer. Some women will feel happier if their partner is there from Day 1. I always felt happy on my own. It gave me the freedom to do whatever I wanted, at the speed I wanted.

If you are with a partner, it is really important that they understand (a) your ability level and (b) your fears. Have the conversation! It is horrendous when someone casually leads you down a road that includes a nightmarish element. I speak from bitter experience!

If that happens, you will handle it, but learning through fear is never the best way. Our brains remember traumatic experiences more vividly than pleasant ones. This is because the job of your brain is to keep you alive. 'Bad' experiences are therefore more useful. The information is kept for future use.

If you are constantly facing unpleasant moments, your body will register the cortisol rushes and start to associate riding with danger. This will manifest as anxiety every time you ride out.

Conversely, if your learning is well-managed and rewarding, your body will fill with all the happy hormones. That is when riding becomes pure pleasure.

Keeping a Journal

If you really want to get better at riding, you need to practise, practise, practise. A short ride every day is ideal.

You also need to focus on your training and ride with purpose. Every instructor I have trained with has said this. It's great fun to ride out with others, but riding alone is best for focussed training. It allows you to be completely single-minded. Whenever I did a junction badly, I immediately went round the block and did it again. I also began each ride out with a twenty minute warm-up on the industrial estate.

I wouldn't have done that with a partner. I would have been worried they were getting bored or impatient.

My journal helped me set goals and mark my progress. At the end of every ride or lesson, I would write down my thoughts and anything I'd learned that was useful. I drew plans of the Mod 1 test site and marked where I needed to accelerate or change gear. I drew endless u-turn boxes, with lines showing where I needed to be looking to get the turning circle right!

I also reflected on the day and what I needed to practise. That would become the focus for my next ride-out eg *Today I am going to focus on roundabouts*.

Some might feel this is all *way* too much. It's over-thinking. Making it seem more of a challenge than it really is.

Some days I share that opinion. That's the honest truth. But I also know we all learn in different ways. I am very methodical. I like to break things down into steps. I like to make lists. I get flustered if people try to hurry me along when I am trying to go through a process - it makes me anxious.

I think we need to learn in our own way, at our own pace. And we are the ones who know what those things are.

Blog Post, October 2021

I have been having a bit of a confidence crisis recently, with my IC (Inner Critic) telling me I wasn't getting better as a rider.

But this morning, I was on a ring road with long queues snaking between the roundabouts. Instantly I pulled out and began filtering, on and on and on past dozens of cars. Then I passed a rider with L plates, sitting patiently in the queue. Nothing wrong with that - I sat in plenty of queues when I was learner. Filtering requires skill, confidence and nerve.

But as I rode on, I realised that I am making progress. I am happy to filter.

This is what I will be putting in my journal tonight. So on those days, when my IC is jabbering, I can re-read and find proof of my progress.

Well Done Me!

It's very easy to come home from a ride telling yourself off for something you messed up.

You cornered badly, you stalled, you were going so slow someone beeped you.... Many of us have a tendency to focus on the negative, rather than the positive.

It isn't helpful. There are *always* little things you can celebrate. Focus on them instead.

I often made a Well Done Me list to help me do this. Here's one of mine. You can see, there's nothing massive here. They are all small achievements. But they *are* achievements. Little by little, I was making progress, and it is really beneficial to have proof of that.

I liked to use different coloured felt pens for my lists, and I always added a few silver stars. When it was finished, I would stick it on my fridge where I could see it.

This might sound a bit too childish for some of you, but I enjoyed being playful and creative, and it really did help me.

The example above is still on my kitchen wall, three years after writing it. It still gives me a warm feeling to read it, especially on those days when I've messed something up again!

> **Well Done Me!**
> - Got bike on and off centre stand TWICE
> - Did Stockwell Hill !!!
>   - 25% ascent
>   - appalling road surface
>   - hill start and stop
> - Didn't go into neutral once by mistake :)
> - Handled wind
> - Didn't grab at front brake
> - Dropped shoulder and did a great u-turn

Lie of the Land

In Google Maps, you can switch to Satellite view and zoom in to the extent you can see lane markings. It's great if you have to ride to somewhere unfamiliar. You can compare routes in advance and decide which suits you best, study difficult junctions and find landmarks to help you navigate (*Past Sainsbury's then get into the right-hand lane, ready for the junction…*)

The only thing it doesn't show is gradients. This has caught me out a few times! Switch to Terrain view to check that out. It's impossible to generalise, but I find that the steepest, bendiest hill roads are between woods rather than arable fields.

If you know there is a hill, you can switch to Street view and ride along the road virtually. As a learner, I did this with a local hill called Sun Rising Hill. I set it as my challenge for the day but checked it out first on Street view. It was a bit scary to see how steep it was, but it really helped me to know there was a sharp bend to the right at the foot of the hill and then an even sharper one to the left at the top. Knowing this meant I was ready with the revs when I reached that more challenging second bend.

Incidentally, the brain cannot tell the difference between riding a route virtually and doing it for real: it is all practise. This is why visualisation works so well for athletes. They can run the perfect race over and over again while lying on a sofa. It will work for you too.

Using Visualisation

- Set yourself a challenge destination and build in a reward at the end of it. Maybe a garden centre nearby that has a good coffee shop, or a trip to a retail park where there's something small you want to buy.

- Find somewhere quiet to sit or lie down. Close your eyes. Breathe deeply.

- Try to picture the route to this place, exactly as you have seen it as a car driver or passenger. Road by road, junction to junction.

- Run this private movie as many times as you need.

- Do the trip for real. It will feel far more familiar to your brain. Remember to buy yourself that reward!

Belly of the Whale

Sometimes it can feel like you're not making any progress at all. If you feel like this, imagine you are in the belly of a whale. It feels like you are stuck, trapped, going nowhere. But the whale is moving. You are going forward, even if it doesn't feel like it.

Keeping a journal really helps with this feeling too. If you read past entries, you will see how far you've come.

'Help! I have been riding for six months and it still feels unnatural'

Many women dream of freedom. Getting on their bike and heading off into the sunshine for carefree rides along country lanes. When this doesn't happen, it's common to question whether it will ever feel 'natural.'

Perhaps I'm not cut out for this?

Instead of that carefree ride, you can spend the whole time praying you will get home safely. (I well remember the overwhelming sense of relief as I turned into my road and parked up at the end of every run) You can feel exhausted with the mental and physical effort of it all, like you've done the whole ride holding your breath.

The truth is, it can take a *very* long time for it to feel natural. I was thousands of miles into my full licence before I stopped talking myself through every roundabout. I still religiously remind myself 'look up' every time I stop at a junction. My instructor Laura told me it takes five-six years for cornering to feel natural.

If you are new to all this and struggling to feel 'at ease,' don't worry. You will get there, in time. In *your* time.

In the meantime, be kinder to your brain. It is doing a great job! It is:

- Working hard to remember multiple processes at the same time.

- Staying vigilant. Its job is to keep you alive. That is why it's not feeling 'carefree.' It is aware you are in a potentially dangerous situation.

- Observing the road. It is (understandably) working in Threat mode. It's dangerous out there!

Practise, practise, practise. Increase your road experience and your confidence will build with it.

Those dreams of carefree riding along country lanes will come true, sooner than you think. Stick with it!

Making mistakes

You cannot move forward without making mistakes. Learning takes place when you move beyond your comfort zone to try new things.

There are two golden rules to remember with mistakes;

1. Don't beat yourself up about it. Everyone makes mistakes. It's part of being human. Be kinder to yourself.

2. Learn from it. Take some time to sit quietly and look at what went wrong.

Why did it happen? Were you going too fast, looking in the wrong place, not paying attention - what? How could you do it differently next time?

I Will Handle It

You might not believe it at the moment, but you will reach a stage where you don't need to do route planning, visualisation or anything else I've just mentioned. You will simply be able to ride out, confident that you will handle anything that comes your way.

Because you *will* handle it. We are all stronger than we think. We handle all kinds of dreadful things that come our way, from divorce to bereavement to illness. We get on with it.

Riding a motorcycle can be scary and stressful, but it is not in the same league as any of these other horrors.

Ultimately, there's only one thing you need to tell yourself before you go out on a ride:

I Will Handle It

The Magic 7

It depends on your work and family commitments, of course, but I found the best times of day to practise on my 125 were 7am and 7pm.

My local housing estate was always quiet at 7am. There would be a couple of dog walkers and an occasional jogger, but hardly any cars would be moving. That all began at 8am, along with the families walking to school. I had a clear hour to practise.

At 7pm, the commuters were home and the roads were amazingly clear. I would ride out into the countryside and have it to myself.

The morning and evening rush hours are dangerous - fact. When it comes to insurance, your premium will be higher if you ride daily during these times. In the morning, no one seems to be fully concentrating. Side-swipes are commonplace, car to car. In the evening, people are impatient to get home so push harder.

According to Direct Line insurance, the most dangerous time to be on the road (for all drivers) is between 5 - 6 pm, especially on a Friday.

'Help! My 125 is sitting in the garage…'

If you're not using your 125, you need ask yourself why. Be honest. Once you know the reason, you can take action.

- If you don't feel confident about riding alone, consider joining a women's group like Curvy Riders (see **Resources**) or post something on a women's page. Are there are any learners locally who would welcome a riding buddy?

- If you don't feel confident handling the bike, consider further one-to-one training. Many schools offer this. Also be honest about the bike. Is it too tall for you? Does it feel too top heavy? Do you feel too 'stretched' to relax? Consider changing the bike.

- Do you *really* want to ride? It can take a long time to get to the stage where you can ride feeling free as a bird. Are you prepared to put in the time and practise needed? If not, maybe it is time to move on (see **The End of the Road**)

Should I do DAS and buy a bigger bike? Would this help?

You can reach a stage where you fall out of love with your 125. It's like a romance: after the fireworks fade and you settle into a routine, it can start to feel boring. You start to see limitations. A 125 can feel like hard work. I had to kick mine to get up hills. Overtaking was usually impossible. Even on dual carriageways a faster overtaker would soon be on my tail light.

I was shocked to find I had fallen out of love with my beautiful 125, but I had outgrown her. That was when I began DAS.

I was hungry to progress. To learn more. To tackle new challenges. I could not do that without moving up.

Do you have that hunger?

A big bike is wonderful but it is not the 'fix all' some people suggest. They can feel easier to ride because they are more stable, but that doesn't make them easy to ride. They are much heavier to manually handle and park, and some women find the extra power scary.

Passing your full licence is just another beginning. The real learning comes afterwards - years of it.

Doing DAS and buying a bigger bike will cost thousands of pounds. It might bring the excitement back into your marriage with motorcycling but maybe it won't.

PART 5: RIDING SOLO

The Joy of Riding Solo

Lessons aside, I have always ridden solo. As a singleton, I have a simple choice: ride alone or don't ride at all. Since passing my Mods and buying a big bike, I have joined a local women's group and enjoyed rides out, but I didn't want to do that as a learner on a 125. It's that female thing of not wanting to hold people up, be in the way, why would they want me blah blah blah!

Some women's rides definitely *do* welcome 125s though, so I had no excuse.

When I began joining online women's groups, I was astounded how often I heard the words 'my hubby' or 'my other half.' I started to feel envious.

I read of partners fixing bikes, buying bikes, picking up fallen bikes, pushing unwisely-parked bikes, lending big bikes for car park practice sessions, riding out on training rides... Through my Singleton Goggles there seemed no end to the advantages of having a partner who rides.

But this is only half the story, of course. So if you are single - REJOICE! There are many advantages to riding alone.

Basically they all come down to freedom. Glorious, shiny freedom.

You are free to take whatever route you want and stop wherever you want, for as long as you want.

You can always go at the speed that suits you.

You can practise for as long as you want. I once did a solid hour of u-turns on my local industrial estate, went for a ride, then returned and did *another* hour. I know myself well enough to say that if I had been with someone else, I would have done fifteen minutes then said I was done, fearing they were getting bored.

You don't pick up bad habits. When did your partner pass their test? How much do they actually know about the tests you will be facing? Many seasoned riders passed their test when examiners stood on the pavement, watched you ride away and waited for you to return fifteen minutes later. They didn't do anything remotely like a Mod 1 course.

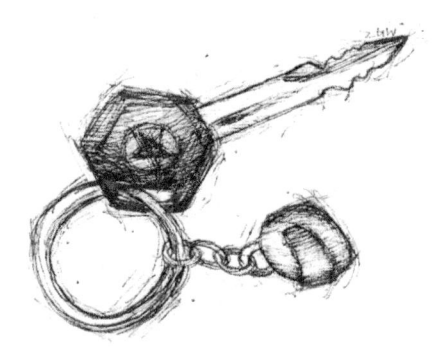

Why don't more women ride solo?

For many women, fear is the issue. Break down on your bike and you are standing there, alone and vulnerable at the side of the road.

I remember listening to the legendary Elspeth Beard at an adventure bike festival. Elspeth was one of the first English women to ride a motorbike around the world. A woman asked her if she was ever afraid.

'There will always be fear,' she replied. 'You just have to get on with it.'

I think it's the same with riding solo. All you can do is ignore the voice that is jabbering away in your head, creating endless fantasy scenarios to persuade you that it is A Very Bad Idea.

True Life Tales: June's Story

I read June's post on a women's page.

'I am thinking of buying a satnav,' she wrote. 'At the moment I can only go where I know and it is boring.'

I can only go where I know... I was fascinated by those words.

Once I had found my confidence, I began to explore my local area. I am lucky: I live on the northern edge of the Cotswolds, so there is a never-ending supply of little lanes to explore. Whenever I was out on my 125 and saw a lane I hadn't been down, my response was usually to turn into it.

I wrote to June to find out more. I discovered she had a full licence, so legally she could go anywhere. She was the one limiting herself.

'Why don't you go further?' I asked.

'Confidence,' she replied. I could almost hear her sigh. 'I'm worried about things going wrong when I'm on my own. I've had the bike six months, but I'm barely using it.'

So many of us have a tendency to focus on the *worst* possible outcome. Punctures, accidents, break downs, getting lost...

But turn it around. What could the *best* possible outcome be? Make a list.

- I'll have a brilliant time.
- I'll have an adventure.
- I'll see something fabulous.
- I'll achieve something and be proud of myself.
- Nothing will go wrong.

Sometimes, when I head off down country lanes, I find unexpected challenges. Steep hills, gravelly surfaces, fords... Once I found myself descending a steep lane that was covered in mud with water running down the centre. I was on it before I realised. No chance to turn back. Talk about buttons being pushed!

But I remember two things about that moment. Firstly, the lane was muddy because I had just passed a farm that had rare longhorn cattle in a yard right next to the road. They were glorious. Seeing them made me feel like I had been whizzed back in time to a medieval village.

And secondly, I handled it. I took it slow, didn't fall off and rode on with a joyous sense of achievement.

It was definitely not boring! I felt deliciously alive.

A final word on getting lost. What is 'lost' ? We live on an island. You're not going to end up in Italy, no matter how far you ride. You won't ride beyond civilisation.

Take a phone, a credit card and your breakdown card and you're set for anything!

> 'THERE'S SOMETHING VERY APPEALING ABOUT GETTING TO KNOW A SMALL AREA WELL'
>
> **Chris Scott, overland adventure biking legend**

Confidence Hack: Running out of Petrol

Some bikes don't have petrol gauges. Instead they have warning lights that come on when your fuel starts to run low. But how low is low? I have been stressed-out over this one plenty of times!

The solution is this. Your bike will have a trip counter - a button that can be pressed to record the number of miles you have done on a trip.

1 Fill up your tank and set this counter to zero. Start riding and make a note of the mileage when the warning light comes on. Remember this figure.

2 Return your counter to zero every time you fill up.

This will help ease your anxiety over running out. You can refuel before the warning light even comes on.

Also bear in mind that the warning light usually means you have 30+

miles of fuel still in the tank. Unless you're out in the wilds, that is plenty of time to find a filling station.

Carry an Emergency Kit

What would help you feel more prepared when riding solo?

I am someone who never goes on holiday without needles and thread, a pair of scissors, fuse wire (fantastically handy) a magnifying mirror, plasters, a clip-on reading light and a wild assortment of pills and potions.

So predictably, I always have a £20 note in my top box in case I forget/lose my purse. On a day's ride-out, a full tank of petrol would get me home.

I also have a spare AA card and the business card of my local bike garage - they do SOS motorcycle recovery.

Many women carry a puncture repair kit (I like the idea but I am not sure I would know how to use it) One of my friends carries emergency flapjacks.

The AA and the emergency services can roughly locate you using your phone but some people like to have the What3Words app on their phone too. Every 3 metre square of the world has been given a unique combination of three words. If you go into the app, it brings up a map of where you are and gives you the three words that pin-point your *exact* location. You can give these words to the emergency services to help them find you quicker.

I learned this tip from Biker Down (see **Biker Down**) It can be useful if you are at the scene of an accident and have to call an ambulance for someone.

Make sure you keep your phone safe (see **Protect Your Phone**) and consider carrying a power pack on a long trip.

Emergency Help From Women's Pages

If you find yourself stranded for whatever reason, it is worth posting something on women's pages straightaway. Someone local might pick it up and offer instant help. I have seen it happen, several times. A woman rider will come out herself, or her hubby will come with a trailer, or she'll give the number of a nearby garage that can help. Even if there's no immediate help, you will get loads of messages of support so you won't feel quite so alone.

You are part of a biking family now and other members will be keen to help. Remember that!

Keep your bike serviced

Blog Post, July 2021

I had my 125 serviced the other day. I've had it a year and ridden 4000 miles, so I reckoned it was due an oil change, at least.

What I hadn't reckoned on was how good I felt when I took her for a spin afterwards.

Maybe it was because my chain came off a few days ago.

I was pootling along a country lane at the time, doing no more than thirty, so it honestly felt no worse than a bicycle shedding its chain. There was an almighty clunking sound my speed dropped instantly and it felt like I was riding a bag of spanners. Instinct told me to pull over and stop, which I did easily enough.

I phoned the AA and waited. It was a blistering hot day, a Bank Holiday, so I knew the wait was going to be a long one. I had no shade and no water with me, and this honestly seemed more important as I settled down by the side of the road to wait. I pulled out my phone and posted a photo on Facebook with a laugh emoji. It was only when the comments started coming that I learned how dangerous losing the chain had been. At speed the loose chain can whip wildly, jamming the wheel or ripping into your leg. With a sickening jolt, I remembered I had been doing fifty on a busy dual carriageway just an hour earlier.

The AA man told me the chain was loose because it was so worn, it couldn't be fully tightened.

The truth was, it could all have been avoided. That service was overdue, as was my MOT, which had expired without my noticing. A chain that worn would not have passed the MOT.

In the Mod 2, you have to answer various 'show and tell' questions. In my lessons, I had confidently talked about chain tension and condition but actually had no real sense of what a 'bad' chain looked like.

After my service, it felt wonderful to know that the tyres were sound the brakes would work if needed and the (new) chain wouldn't fall off mid-ride!

Have Breakdown Assistance

When the chain came off, it was fantastic to be able to call the AA. I was alone, as usual. A passing biker stopped to see if I was alright. He managed to get the chain back on but didn't have the necessary tools to tighten it, so I couldn't ride home. Well maybe I could, but it would have been at a very slow speed, with me stressing-out all the way.

When the AA man arrived, he told me he was a biker himself. This reassured me he knew what he was doing, which sounds crazy when I say it now, but that is how our heads work sometimes. *The AA fix cars... but can they fix bikes?* The answer is yes. He told me that all patrol people are trained to fix bikes as well as cars.

Check your policy. If your roadside assistance comes free as part of a package (with your house insurance, for example) make sure it covers a motorcycle. I have heard of women being stranded because they've discovered their cover applied only to the main family car.

How To Enjoy A Solo Ride

RIDE WITH PURPOSE:
A DESTINATION, A GOAL,
A MEETING

FOCUS ON THE BEST POSSIBLE
OUTCOME (NOT THE WORST)

DRESS FOR THE WEATHER

PART 6: RIDING WITH OTHERS

Riding with a friend or partner

Since writing **The Joy of Riding Solo** (and passing my Mods) I have found a local riding buddy and I have to say, I really like it. I find it reassuring to have someone there in case something goes wrong. If I cannot manoeuvre the bike out of a parking space, he helps me (though to be fair, this is usually because he has led me into a parking place I could see was going to be trouble!)

When he leads, he takes me down roads I might not otherwise have ridden, and the challenge of them is improving my skills.

We always set a destination, so it never feels like riding aimlessly.

I asked a group of women riders for advice on riding with a partner or friend. Here is what they said:

'Ride staggered. Nothing worse than just being able to see the bum of the rider in front. Also gives more braking distance for the unexpected and leaves less gap for cars to get in between you and be a pain.'

'Ride your own ride. If not comfortable, don't speed up to keep up with them.'

'Always agree the route and destinations before departure. Saves a domestic at some point in the day!'

'I like using intercom to discuss route, hazards in road, oncoming cars on narrow bends, etc…as long as concentration is maintained.'

'Agree a meeting point when you're riding together, so no pressure on either one of you if you get split up.'

'If no comms, agree set hand signals, for things like need petrol, need pee stop, need drink, numb bum.'

'Enjoy the time together. Try not to get stressed if they do something with minimal warning.'

Group riding

Blog Post, May 2022

Yesterday I did my first group ride, riding with five sisters from the Curvy Riders Motorcycling Club. We rode to Goodrich Castle, in celebration of International Female Ride Day.
I loved it! Found it thrilling.
It was challenging at junctions. To keep the group together, the leader waited for a gap big enough for all the riders to get through. So I had to be prepared to stop, even if my instinctive decision was to go. It was the same with overtaking. I could see a gap but it was the leader's call as to whether it was big enough for everyone to overtake safely.
Riding with the group gave me reassurance - they would never leave a sister behind - and challenges. Especially when the leader missed the castle entrance and led us up a steep winding hill, with no alternative at the top but to turn around and ride back down!!

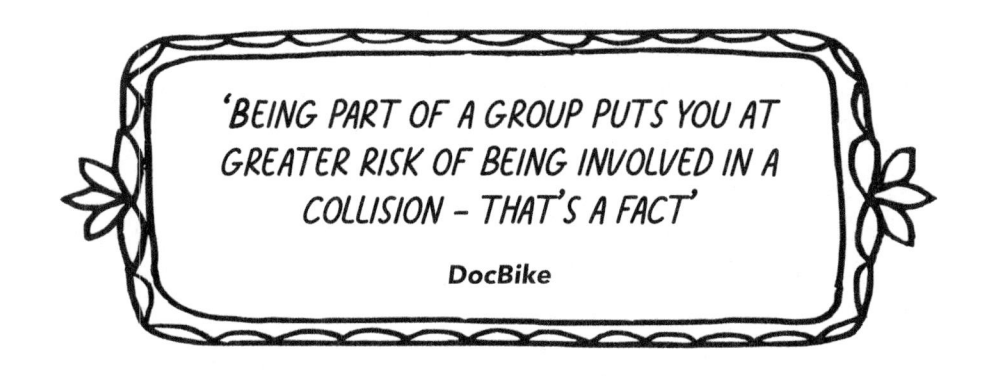

> 'BEING PART OF A GROUP PUTS YOU AT GREATER RISK OF BEING INVOLVED IN A COLLISION - THAT'S A FACT'
>
> **DocBike**

Group riding is exhilarating but risky. That's what DocBike says, and they should know. DocBike is a charity that sends out highly trained critical care doctors and paramedics on response motorcycles to save lives.

Recently I went out on an advanced ride with ten other riders. It was fabulous, Everyone knew exactly where they should be in relation to the others. We moved as one, like a flock of starlings.

Sadly this is not always the case. This is why group riding can be risky. *You* might be disciplined when it comes to road positioning but others might not. Some riders might be fast but not especially skilful. I once rode with a guy who repeatedly cut across my path. He didn't stop doing it even when I asked him to stop. I needed my wits about me that day!

I have only done a handful of group rides so far, so I asked online for advice from more experienced women riders. Here are some of the things they said.

Ride your own ride. Definitely the #1 advice. Don't ride any faster than you are comfortable with. If the rider in front overtakes, don't go for the gap they used - it might have closed up by the time you get there.

Ride staggered. They all mentioned this too. If you're riding in one long line and suddenly have to stop, you can slam into the backside of the bike in front (or have someone do it to you) Staggering gives everyone room but also enables the group to keep together when riding through busy areas.

Ride towards the front of the group if you're a slow rider. Inevitably groups become stretched out. It's easier for the more experienced ones to catch up so they are better further down the line.

Keep an eye on the person behind you. Slow down a little if you're losing them. This will help the stretching problem. (Some would say the exact opposite to this - it is up to the person behind to keep up. You see why it gets complicated?)

Talk to the ride organiser before setting out. In some groups, the unspoken rule might be 'don't overtake other riders.' In others, safe overtaking might be acceptable. Every group is different and it is much better to know in advance how others might ride.

Check how hard the ride will be. Some weekend rides can be four or five hours of hard riding. That's great if you're a seasoned rider, but as a newbie, I find that too long to be enjoyable. There's more mental effort needed when you're still learning. I don't enjoy riding when I'm exhausted and my hands are cramping. How many stops will there be? What is the route? The destination? How long is it likely to take? Find out in advance. If you needed to head home halfway through, would you know the way? Consider running your own GPS, even if you're following someone.

Fill up your tank and go to the toilet. Two reasons why many rides start at petrol stations! It can be really annoying for others if you need to stop or detour for fuel along the way. Make sure your bike is in a good condition.

If you can't go, tell the organiser as soon as you know. Make sure you have their phone number in case you break down on the way to the meeting place.

A good ride leader will stop frequently to make sure everyone is still with the group and feeling happy. They will ride in lead position throughout the ride and there should also be a 'tail-end Charlie' at the very end of the group. They are there to make sure no one gets lost or left behind.

Everyone else rides between these two riders. Some rides use what is known as the 'second person drop-off system.' It works like this:

The leader is in number 1 position. When the group comes to a place where the route is unclear or changes from 'straight ahead' the leader will indicate to show the way. The rider in the number 2 position pulls up somewhere safe at the side of the road and indicates which way the leader has gone ie if the leader has turned left at a junction, number 2 will park up before the junction with their indicator flashing 'left.'

Once all the riders are past (except the tail-end Charlie) rider 2 joins the end of the line. Now there is a new number 2.

Some women refuse to ride in groups they don't know because it can be frustrating and dangerous. Some of the fastest riders are the least skilful. This includes women. Never assume women riders will be sensible. Plenty of would-be Valentino Rossis are female. You won't know who is a problem until you are out on the road with them.

If you're on a 125, check with the organiser that it's okay for you to join the ride. Sometimes routes can involve motorways.

Interestingly, my instructor Laura is against learners riding their 125s alongside bigger bikes. Read her interview (at the end of the book) to learn more.

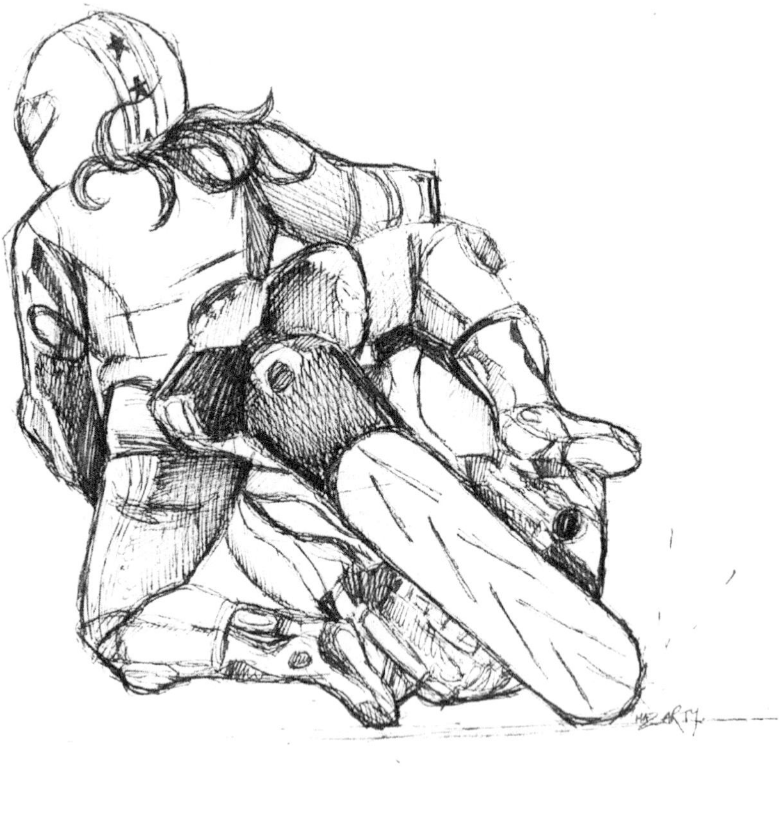

PART 7: PARKING AND MANUAL HANDLING

Car parks can be very difficult for a beginner. Supermarket car parks, retail parks.... People are very distracted, whether they are on foot or in their cars, so you have to take it at walking pace, which is challenging for a learner. Stalling is common, and there's nothing wrong with that.

There can also be *very* tight turns. On my 125, I was shocked at how tight the roundabout into my local retail park was. I think nothing of it in the car: *go left into the park, turn right at the mini roundabout…*

But that right hand turn took me by surprise, I don't mind admitting. It was one of those moments when I could only hold on and remind myself to look where I wanted to go!

Nipping to the shops to get something is one of the loveliest jaunts you can do as a beginner. There's something deeply satisfying about having the destination and the purpose then returning triumphantly with the booty, mission accomplished.

If you are prone to panicking or getting overwhelmed, run through the trip in your head before you get there. How exactly do you get in to that retail park? If there are traffic lights, what lane will you need to be in?

Petrol Stations

This one is easy, riding with a partner. You pull in behind them, unscrew your cap and they fill up both bikes, no problem. But doing it alone can be a nerve-shredding experience, especially the first time. One woman told me she was so anxious about filling up her new 125, she bought a petrol can from Amazon, drove her car to the garage to fill it then put the petrol into her bike in the privacy of her garage.

Petrol stations are a tricky combination of slow control, tight turns and stopping. Spillages can make you nervous about skidding. Car drivers can pressure you to hurry up when moving off, and everyone seems to be watching you. (You definitely get watched more as a woman. You're a novelty)

Being prepared can help with nerves.

Using a Petrol Station for the First Time

Practise opening and closing the fuel cap *before* you go to the petrol station. They can be surprisingly tricky. The first time I went with my 125, I found I couldn't open it for the life of me. After five minutes of fiddling, I started asking random strangers for help. They couldn't do it either. I was there fifteen minutes before a biker pulled in and showed me how it was done. I felt a right donut.

You will see more experienced riders sitting on their bikes to fill up. This enables them to get more fuel into the tank. As a beginner, It's always safer to put the side stand down and dismount before attempting to fill your tank.

The petrol flow will stop automatically when it reaches a certain level - you can't overfill.

Do I need to take off my helmet?

Increasingly, riders are being told to remove their helmets before they can fill up. A voice will ring out over the tannoy as you stand at the pump, wondering why it isn't working.

It feels unfair and embarrassing. You had no intention of driving off without paying, and the car drivers aren't being singled out.

So why you?

Curiously, it isn't about petrol theft. It's an attempt to tackle bike theft.

Bikes are stolen to be sold but also to be used by gangs as getaway bikes. If the rider keeps their helmet on as they fill up, the CCTV captures the number plate, but the thief cannot be identified.

It's not the garage that is telling you to take off your helmet; the garage has been instructed by the police to insist on it.

Can I jump ahead of queuing cars?

This is a thorny topic! Some people say yes, others say definitely no. Personally, I would do it if:

    a. There was a car filling up at a pump but the car at the pump in front of them had gone and

b. The gap was too small for a car to squeeze through.

My tank fills up so quickly, I can be in the shop while the car behind me is still finishing.

It is generally agreed that the one time it is *not* advisable to do this is when fuel is running short and people are panic buying. When tempers are fraying, you don't want to be on the receiving end of it.

Being hassled by the car behind

Let's face it, it can take time to get your gloves back on, your visor down and your wits gathered, ready to pull off safely with cars all around. It's no longer than some drivers take, with their phone checking, coffee sipping and seat belt fastening, but they are cocooned in metal. You are fully exposed to the impatience of the car driver behind.

What can you do to ease this?

Carry your debit card in your jacket pocket. You don't want to be fiddling with unlocking and re-locking your top box to get your purse then doing it all again once you've paid.

Take your gloves with you and put them back on in the shop. (Winter gloves can be especially fiddly with straps!) Same if you want to adjust anything on your jacket, check your route or whatever. You can't be hassled in the shop.

Don't meet the gaze of the driver. Get on the bike, take a deep breath and go when you're ready.

Biker Cafes

Pulling in at biker cafes can be really daunting. Always there are guys standing around, watching each new bike that rolls up. You have to stop and park, in front of them all. *Aaargh…!* Even experienced males have told me they hate doing it.

Dropping your bike would be deeply embarrassing, right? But here's the truth of it: you would have *instant* help. Bikers are very kind to other bikers. They wouldn't laugh - they would help. Your bike would be picked up and checked over.

It's the same with parking. I went on my own to a biker cafe that had an appalling car park. It was gravel and had a steep downhill gradient. Running late, I abandoned my bike where I stopped, knowing there would be problems later. Sure enough, when I returned to the car park I saw every other bike had been parked facing uphill when mine was facing downhill.

I didn't have the confidence to attempt a downhill u-turn (on gravel!) So I sat on her and tried edging down, feet on the ground, hand on the front brake, jerking, jerking. I was terrified. So I climbed off and tried the same thing but pushing. Again terrifying and *so* slow.

I put down the side stand and approached the nearest group of bikers. There was a big bear of a guy, all in black leather, with tattoos and a great long beard.

'I am sorry to bother you,' I said. 'But would you mind moving my bike for me? I'm scared I'm going to drop it.'

'Sure,' he said, with a smile. He took hold of the handlebars, effortlessly swung her round, climbed on, rode her out of the car park and parked her on the road, facing exactly where I needed to go.

'Thank you *so much*,' I said when I joined him.

'No problem,' he said. 'We've all been there. Always happy to help.'

Honestly, if I hadn't asked him to help, I would still be there now!

Biker cafes can be great fun - I encourage you to try them, even on your own. It's not difficult to strike up a conversation. 'Have you come far?' or 'This is a handsome bike' might sound tired here on the page, but they work well in real life, believe me. It's not like being at a cocktail party where you have no idea who people are or what they might be interested in. Bikers love to talk about their bikes!

As a beginner, it can be a good place to ask for mechanical advice too. I remember asking someone to show me how a disk lock worked. I was thinking of buying one but had no real idea what one was, I explained. He happily gave me a demonstration.

Confidence Hack: Parking Alongside Bigger Bikes

Feeling daunted, rolling up on a 125 with L plates when everyone else is riding a beast? You can always defuse it with a joke. If I felt eyes were on me as I dismounted, I used to say 'Stand back - the big bikes are arriving.' It always brought a smile and worked well as an entry into a chat with strangers.

Gravel, Gravel Everywhere

Cafes and garden centres make great destinations when you're looking to ride out somewhere. Unfortunately, their parking areas were designed for cars and sometimes this means gravel.

Gravel is *not* nice to ride on, and stopping on it can be a bit skiddy. It's easy to slip and go down.

If you're unsure about a new cafe, ask online what the car park is like. I find Curvy Riders invaluable for this because membership is organised into local groups. I guarantee someone in your area will be able to tell you (a) what the car park's like and (b) the quality and range of the cakes on offer! (See **Resources**)

The Perils of Paddling

You might have seen people 'paddling' their bikes? That's when you sit on the bike, put both feet down and push the bike into (or out of) a space backwards.

I confess I do it myself when I am getting my bike out of the garage.

But it is neither advised nor encouraged by instructors, simply because it is very easy to drop the bike in this position. All it takes is one slip of the foot and you can be down. Try doing it on a gravel car park or on a smooth car park in the rain and you will see exactly what I mean. If you are doing it on tip-toes, it's even riskier. And once a bike is going down, it's going down. All you can do is try not to go down with it.

The safest way to move a bike is by pushing it. That is why it is a requirement of the Mod 1 test.

Filtering

Filtering is a major heart-thumper for a lot of women. The main anxiety is being stranded on the wrong side of the road with no space to get into and traffic coming the other way.

But staying put often brings a different kind of stress, as we tell ourselves off for being wussy.

Filtering is something you build up to. It takes time. Not only does it take skill - you need perfect balance and *must* be able to control the throttle - it takes confidence and nerve. You also need the ability to scan the road ahead while keeping a close eye on the cars immediately in front of you.

Do you still do car park practice? It is the only way to get better at things like this. Filtering is slow control, the same as you do in Mod 1. Go to a car park and practise, practise, practise.

There are two kinds of filtering:

- In and out filtering, where you overtake a couple of slow-moving cars at a time then nip into an available space before doing it again

- Long filtering, where there's a long queue and you ride past everything, occasionally nipping into a space or pausing alongside a car. Often this is done between lines of traffic, making it a tight fit.

Long filtering is easier, but you must take it slowly. You should not be going more than 15-20 mph faster than the slow traffic. Ignore the idiots who whizz through at sixty on motorways. Car and van drivers *do* open doors - I have seen it happen. Maybe they're eating a pasty and decide to brush the crumbs off their lap. Why not? They're not going anywhere. *BANG*.

Other hazards to look out for are

- vehicles changing lanes without looking - the driver has eyes only for the space that has suddenly become available

- drivers suddenly deciding to do a u-turn to escape the jam. They can cut right across your path.

You need to be super-vigilant. Always be prepared to stop. You also need to know the width of your bike, especially if you're carrying panniers.

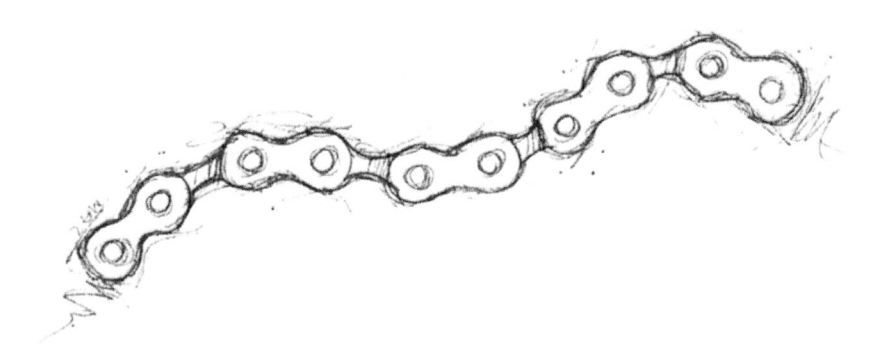

What if I don't get a space?

I find cars very accommodating. They generally give me a space if I need one. This opens up all kinds of debates on whether drivers are more courteous to women (or just give them a wider berth!) I look very feminine, with blonde hair beneath my helmet and pink flashes on my jacket. Personally, I think this helps. I think I would get a rougher ride filtering if I was a young guy in black leathers.

If you do get stranded, pull in as close as you can to a car and wait for the trouble to pass. That's all you can do. But prevention is always better than cure. Anticipation is key.

Should I follow another rider?

Some say yes, some say no. If you are lacking in confidence, following in the wake of an experienced rider (whether you know them or not) can be the boost you need. I certainly built my confidence by doing this, with complete strangers. But be aware, especially with random passing bikers, that they will be concentrating on their own safety. The gap they pull into might be big enough for one bike, but not two. This is why some women would say no to following.

The Golden Rule for filtering is:

Ride your own ride

You don't have to filter at all. It's your choice. There's no shame in sitting in the queue. If you decide to do it, do it at your speed.

If you are still too nervous to filter, be patient. The confidence will come with time and practice. I don't remember filtering at all on my 125, but I adore doing it on my 650. I get very excited if I am on a motorway and see a jam ahead!

But still, there are times when I will choose not to do it. Usually that is when it's raining; the white lines on a road can get *very* slippy when wet and filtering can mean riding over a lot of lines. If I don't feel I can guarantee 100% control of my bike, I don't do it.

Filtering with partners and groups

Filtering is one area where there can be a big difference between riders. You *must* have this conversation before you set off. In groups, it will be assumed you are willing and able to filter. If you are leading a ride, say with a local woman you have met online, find out how the other woman feels about it. If you are riding with your partner, make it clear how you feel. Set your boundaries. If you are happy to filter in a town but *not* through tunnels of lorries on a motorway, they need to know.

Manual Handling

If you're struggling with this one, you are definitely not alone. Everyone struggles at some stage, especially in the beginning. Bikes are heavy. An average 650cc training bike weighs in at 200kg. That is the same as an upright piano - or an adult dolphin!

The good news is, manual handling is technique + confidence in your ability to do it. These things can be learned and practised.

Weight is something you get used to. My CB125F seemed enormous when I bought her. I would inch her out of her parking space every day during that first summer. But a curious thing happened. Winter came and she sat covered with a rain cover for months. When I started riding again in April, she seemed *much* smaller. Her size wasn't intimidating at all.

Then I did my DAS and used her to practise my manual handling technique. I ended up wheeling her round the car park like she was a push bike!

It was the same with my 650. I learned on a Gladius and remember the sheer weight of her as I eased her upright and found my balance for the first time. Putting her back onto the side stand after a few slow circuits round the car park was terrifying. The stand was down, the instructor was beside me, there was no way she was going to drop, but to feel her dead weight tipping sideways until she settled... yikes.

I ride my own Gladius now. I am used to her weight though I still don't like setting her down onto the side stand! I am also very careful about road cambers. Too often I have parked only to find I can't get her upright again. When that happens, I push her forwards into a better position before climbing on.

Manual handling is one of the elements in the Mod 1 test. Over the course of my training, I saw ten students do the manual handling exercise. The eight men made it look as easy as breathing. The two women were as anxious as I was.

My instructors confirmed, women find it harder and far more daunting. Why? That eternal fear of dropping the bike. Being anxious doesn't help. It tenses muscles that work better when relaxed.

I would watch Laura, my trainer, as she moved the bikes in and out of the parking bays at the school. It clearly had nothing to do with strength and everything to do with technique. She did it so fast, with such ease, one hand on the left handle, the other palm down on the seat. Job done.

In the Mod 1 test, you can do it as slowly as you want. I did it slow and steady and actually did it very well. It gave me a real boost!

I had spent hours practising though, and practice is the key to manual handling. Many women ride *huge* bikes, whether they are super-heavy cruisers or top-heavy adventure bikes. They have learned the technique that suits them, and you can do that too. It's a great feeling when you can move your bike in and out of a parking space with ease, no help needed. That's independence!

Confidence hack: putting a 125 on the centre stand

It can be nerve-wracking when you're trying to learn this, especially if you have no one to help you. It feels like the whole bike could come crashing down if you get it wrong.

I found it helped to park the bike alongside a wall before practising. Then I could do it with confidence, knowing the bike couldn't fall more than a few inches on that far side.

One of the buildings in my local industrial estate was perfect for this.

I also found it was easier to do when wearing gloves. I could grip harder without hurting my hands.

Forgotten the technique?

I had been shown the technique during my CBT but had forgotten it by the time I actually needed to do it (I was putting my bike into winter storage) So I went to my local Honda showroom, explained the situation and a sales guy happily brought out a CB125F to gave me a refresher lesson. He even held it while I practised a few times.

I hadn't bought my bike there; I bought it online. It didn't make any difference, they were still happy to help.

It's worth remembering this if you ever need a bit of help or advice but have no one to turn to.

PART 8: WHATEVER THE WEATHER

Wind

If you're on a 125, the wind can be seriously scary, especially if you are new to riding. By-passes and dual carriageways can be especially challenging, with sideways gusts that push you right across your lane. Simply holding a straight line becomes a battle as you find yourself hanging on for dear life.

Bigger bikes are easier, but they can still take a real buffeting, especially naked bikes. (A naked bike doesn't have fairings. A fairing is a shell placed over the frame of the bike to deflect wind.)

The good news is, you become used to wind. Honestly. Even on a 125.

There are a few things you can do to feel more confident in the wind.

1. Check the weather forecast

Any good weather app will show you the expected wind speeds and what direction the wind will be blowing from. You will soon learn what you feel confident handling. As I recall, anything over 6 was challenging when I was a complete beginner.

Which isn't to say you should stay home if you are confident with 6 but a 7 is forecast. Keep pushing yourself. You will handle it, believe me, and it's wonderful to get home knowing you have just sailed through a higher wind than you've experienced before.

Your weather forecast might also describe the wind. This is useful too. I soon learned there was a difference in feel between a 'gentle breeze,' a 'moderate breeze' and 'light winds.'

2. Relax

The best advice I was ever given was grip with your knees and relax from the waist up. This transformed my riding in the wind. No more holding on for dear life.

3. Remove your top box. This can help stabilise the bike, especially a 125.

4. Reframe

Change the story you are telling yourself. Instead of 'battling the wind,' tell yourself you are 'dancing in the air.' How does that feel now?

Life is easy for a leaf or a dandelion seed, happily held in the breath of the wind. There's no stress, just joy.

This might sound fanciful but it works every time for me. Find an image that works for you. Sometimes I like to imagine the West Wind is playing badminton with the North Wind and I am the shuttlecock!

Rain

I confess, I don't go out for a ride if it's raining. But we all know how changeable the weather can be in the UK. The clouds roll in from nowhere and soon you're caught in a downpour. So you need to be confident with it.

The best advice? Slow down. Braking distances are doubled in the wet (as you learned for your theory test, right?) Painted lines on the road can become incredibly slippery, so avoid them where possible. Drain covers can be troublesome too.

If your bike has Rain Mode, use it. It will ease the ride and offer reassurance.

If the rain is really bad, or you are getting stressy, pull over as soon as you can and wait for the worst to pass. You won't get any medals for struggling on. Seeing a queue forming behind you because your speed is dropping will only add to your anxiety. Sometimes five minutes can make a big difference.

Still anxious? Remember this:

Tyre manufacturers spend millions of pounds testing and developing tyres that will work under all conditions. If rain was impossible to ride in, the streets would be littered with fallen riders whenever it rained.

- Many women commute every day, in all weather, with no mishaps.
- Keep your tyres in good condition, watch your speed and you will get home.

On a long ride, pack a spare base layer and gloves if you have them. If you do get unexpectedly drenched, you'll feel much better if you can change into dry kit once the rain has passed.

If you find your gloves aren't waterproof, wear a pair of thin surgical gloves underneath them. This will help keep your hands dry.

If you're struggling to see because of fog, rain, car spray or insects, a Visorcat can help. It's a wash & wipe system that fits to your glove. It contains a small sponge and you swipe it across your visor in one smooth stroke to wash then swipe back to dry. visorcat.com

Fog

Bikers often feel invisible on the road. Add fog to the mix and that suspicion is confirmed. You can feel *very* vulnerable.

If you have a fluorescent waistcoat, now is the time to put it on. It will make you feel better. If you don't have one, get one. They are very cheap and pack up small - you can keep one in your top-box.

Use dipped headlight only. Full beam will bounce right back at you.

Be aware that your visor can be making things appear worse. Wipe your visor every thirty seconds. If it's really bad, consider riding with the visor up.

Snow, Ice and Frost

I haven't experienced snow or ice. To be honest, the thought of riding with either terrifies me, so I garage my bike through the worst of the winter.

The Highway Code lists the stopping distances at various speeds. In snow and ice, they need to be increased by up to *ten times*. Tyres have virtually no traction; sliding and skidding are very real possibilities. If you use your bike for work, you might have no choice. But the general advice for these conditions is don't ride.

I do have experience of frost. In Italy, on a very sunny morning, I hit an unexpected frost pocket, the bike slid from under me and I found myself on the tarmac with the bike pinning me down (see **My First Tumble**)

If you are tempted to take your bike out on a sunny winter's day, check your weather app to see if it went below freezing in the night. Consider going out later in the day so any frost or ice has time to evaporate. Be very careful on country lanes with overhanging trees where the sun might not penetrate. That is where frost and ice might linger.

There is one such lane near my house. It has a warning sign ahead of it, a black snowflake in a red triangle.

Cold hack: Carry a pair of ordinary tights in your bag. If you start to feel cold, slip them on under your trousers. They make a big difference without adding bulk. Forgotten to bring a pair? Charity shops sell new ones very cheap.

Sunshine

> 'THE SUN TODAY IS EVIL'
> **Rider at Koti Autalli bike cafe**

In my first year of riding, as summer moved into autumn I started to have trouble with low sunshine. If you're a driver, you will know the kind of sun I mean. It's when the sun is hanging low in the sky but still shining bright. It gets you directly in the eyes, making you hit the brake and pull your sun visor down in one swift move.

The problem I found was that I already *had* my sun visor down and it wasn't enough. The sun was shining directly into my eyes.

The first time it happened, I found it *really* scary. It was like riding blind.

The only thing I could think of to fix it was to radically change direction. So I took the next turning and rode home a different way than planned. By the time I had to head back in the direction of the sun, it had dropped lower and was no longer a problem.

Now I am more experienced, I am more prepared for it, but there's still nothing I can do except keep an eye on the clock and avoid roads I know to be prone to it.

Remember drivers will be blinded too. There's every chance they haven't seen you, so keep your speed down and be prepared to stop.

Cold

Being too cold can be a serious distraction. You must have the right clothing for the time of year. Think layers. I carry a base layer on even the warmest of days (I find my summer weight jacket can feel very cold if the sun goes in - it has mesh panels that are permanently open)

If you find you're getting too sweaty using cotton base layers, try running tops and leggings instead. They are lightweight and breathable.

If you are feeling cold, stopping for a cup of tea will help, even if you feel tempted to push on for home. Add sugar, even if you don't usually take it.

Heated handgrips are fantastic. They fit around the handgrips on your handlebars and are wired in to the bike. A flick of the switch and they warm up, warming your hands.

Heat

On hot days, carry water. When I broke down on my 125, my biggest concern was my lack of water. It was blisteringly hot, I was on a rural road and had a two-hour wait for the AA.

Some women like to immerse their tee shirts in cold water before wringing them out and putting them back on. This seems extreme to me, but it works for them!

If you find yourself getting sticky in the saddle, try adding an airflow saddle cover.

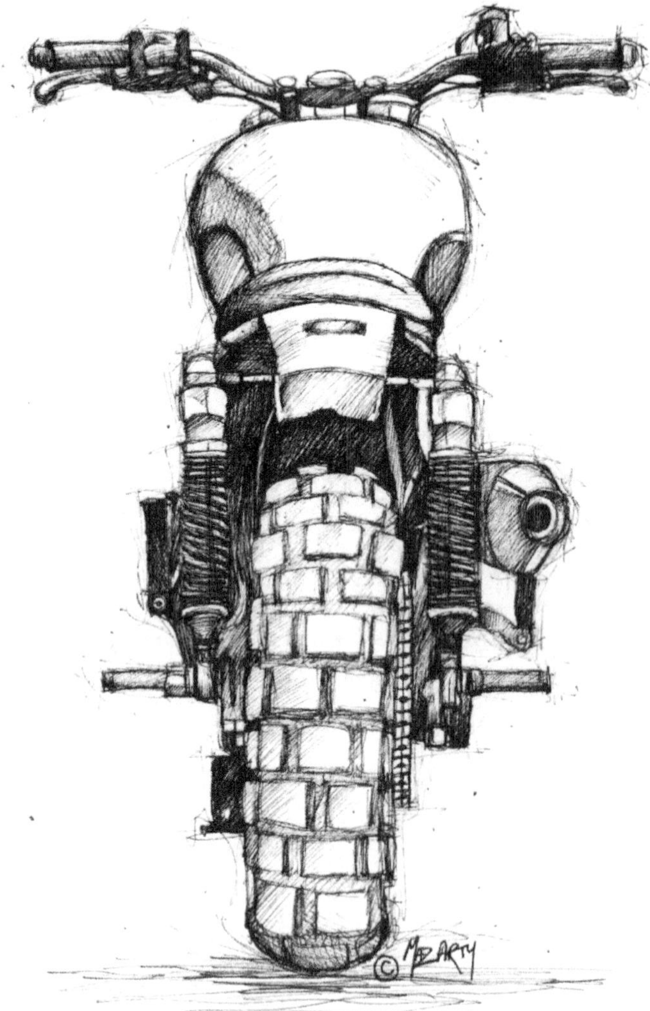

PART 9: MANAGING FEAR AND ANXIETY

> *"WE CANNOT BUBBLE WRAP OURSELVES TO GO THROUGH LIFE"*
>
> **Vanessa Ruck, The Girl on a Bike**

The Sliding Scale

Anxiety doesn't come alone. It comes with a chorus of inner voices that bring you down like a pack of dogs.

'Stop being a wuss / wimp / idiot'

'Get on with it.'

'Stop making a fuss.'

'Just DO it.'

The crazy thing is, you *want* to do it, more than anything else in the world. But you're like a toddler in reins, there's something holding you back.

Anxiety defies logic. It doesn't make sense and you know it doesn't, but still it is there.

So that's what this chapter is about: managing anxiety and fear.

Are they the same thing? Not to me. I feel like they are on a sliding scale. At the lower end, I can feel…

Nervous

Worried

Fretful

Apprehensive

…but they are not the same as anxiety. Anxiety comes with a definite set of physical symptoms. My heart feels like it is going to hammer its way out of my chest. My thinking goes fuzzy and narrow. A bit obsessive - I can only think about the thing that is causing me anxiety. The voice in my head goes into overdrive. My breathing is shallow and rapid. I feel a bit shaky. I have no desire to eat or drink. You can say something to me but I will only half-hear it. I am in a state of panic.

Fear (for me) is something different again. It is located in my head rather than in my body. It is a projection, a narrative. My head is leaping forward into an abyss, fixing on bad outcomes. Physically I will get the thumping heart and rapid breathing, but there is also a cold sense of dread. Something bad is going to happen and my body is preparing to face it.

Feeling nervous about climbing on a bike is usual. It comes and goes with me, very fleeting. I went through a definite stage of bike-related anxiety, feeling it *every time* I took my bike out of the garage. But I can only remember feeling fear once. That was when I tried to ride a bike I had previously crashed on. I was overcome with such a feeling of dread, I went into meltdown and couldn't ride. I honestly felt I was going to die if I rode that bike that day.

So there is a sliding scale. Thankfully I am no longer troubled by bike anxiety, but the chapter is called *Managing* Fear and Anxiety for a reason. We can never truly overcome fear; it is hardwired into our system. It is part of our survival mechanism. It has been there ever since we ran away from mammoths and sabre-toothed tigers.

Just the other day, I chatted to a woman who told me she still had days when she climbed on her bike feeling sick to her stomach with nerves. She had been riding for thirty-six years.

All we can do with fear and anxiety is learn how to handle it.

Dissonance

Dissonance isn't a word much used, but I suspect it's something many women riders struggle with.

Dissonance is disharmony. A lack of agreement. If you feel you are a lion but you're behaving like a mouse, that is dissonance.

The image of a female biker is potent. She's strong, independent, assured, confident, kick-ass, capable, wild, free, stylish, sexy. But as a beginner, you can feel the very opposite of all this.

My anxiety problems kicked in with my 650, not my 125. I would be standing in the garage, fully geared up, wanting to be strong, capable and the rest. That was how I saw myself. That is how I *am*, most of the time. Yet I was trembling as I pulled on my gloves.

The dissonance would make me attack myself. The weakness felt shameful. This wasn't how I wanted to feel. This wasn't how it was meant to be.

Amazingly, I managed to overcome my anxiety (see **WingWave**) Now I climb on my bike feeling strong, capable, assured... I love this version of myself.

Anxiety is like a snapping dog, guarding the gateway to carefree riding. If I can get past it, there's every chance you can get past it too.

I Met An Acrobat

I met an acrobat while I was writing this book. Jade was in her thirties and performed with a male partner, Tom. Their act was highly skilful but comedic - they would achieve a position then Tom would 'drop' her as she tried to dismount.

The drops were formidable. At one point, Tom stretched his arms above his head, Jade stood upright on his hands then fell. Tom caught her in his arms like a bride.

In another move, she fell head first. Tom caught her around her waist before she hit the ground.

So scary.

When I found myself sitting next to Jade at supper, I asked the question that had been burning in my brain.

'How did you conquer your fear?'

'I haven't conquered it,' she said with a smile. 'I feel fear every time. There's one move where I think I am going to die every time.'

That was the head-first drop.

'What do you fear?' I asked. 'Do you fear Tom will drop you, or do you fear you will mess up?'

'Always me,' she said. 'That I will mis-time something and it will go wrong.'

'Yet you still do the act. How?'

'I practise,' she said, 'over and over again until it is in my muscles. And then, if my brain does blimp for a second, the muscles will do the right thing anyway.'

I asked her what was in her head when she did the routine. Was she giving herself commands, like *look up, look up* to help with balance?

'No,' she said. 'I just try to keep very present and relaxed. If I got stressy, my muscles would tense up, which is the last thing I need.'

It's the same for us as it is for Jade. Relax, breathe, stay present, have faith in your training and ability, and trust your partner - your bike.

As learners we need to let go of the idea that the fear will pass. It won't. It will likely be there every time we get on the bike. Fear is often caused by over-thinking, but it is also a primal reaction. Picture the look that comes into a rabbit's eyes when it senses a dog. That is not being caused by over-thinking!

> 'THERE IS ONLY ONE THING WE SAY TO DEATH: 'NOT TODAY.'
>
> **Syrio Forel, Game of Thrones**

Catastrophising

I once told a guy I was worried about dropping my bike at a junction because the vehicle behind me might not stop and then I would be run over.

His face was a picture of puzzlement. 'Seriously?' he said. 'Why on earth would you think that?'

I couldn't explain. Yet I felt that same puzzlement when a woman told me she was worried a wheel might drop off while she was riding.

This is catastrophising. It is spinning a story of what might happen, and it's always a downbeat, worrying story. Your story can defy logic. It makes no sense to anyone except yourself.

But it feels real. That's what fear is -

False

Evidence

Appearing

Real

A tendency to catastrophise can be very limiting. It can make you over-cautious. You will talk yourself out of going to a certain town because you won't be able to find somewhere to park and then you'll be riding round and round and the traffic could be bad and you'll be lost …. and…. *Aargh!*

The best way to deal with this is to

    a. Be vigilant. Recognise that you are catastrophising

    b. In that moment, tell yourself to STOP

    c. Work only with FACTS. Ask yourself: Is that a fact?

So much anxiety is caused by future thinking. This *might* happen.

The solution is to stay in the present. I find it really useful to say to myself:

Is it a problem RIGHT NOW?

If the answer is no, let the fear go. Deal with the object of your fear if - *IF!* - it suddenly appears on the road in front of you.

Always focus on the *best* possible outcome for your ride:

Today I will have a fabulous ride along country lanes ablaze with autumn colours

not

Today I might skid on wet leaves and come off

It's a question of finding a balance between safety and risk. It's true, autumn does bring fallen leaves and they can be slippery. Going out on an autumn day will therefore involve some element of risk. But what a glorious ride it will be through those fiery colours.

Motorcycling will *always* involve risk. But leaving your house involves risk. Staying home involves risk! How many people are injured by ladders and slippers every year? We need to be aware of the risks and ride accordingly.

We need to ride!

Trust your brakes

When I did a Biker Down course, one of the traffic police leading the course (Phil) told us he had only recently returned to riding after having a broken leg. It was his mate who had broken it for him.

His mate was newly qualified. They were out riding together when something unexpectedly blocked their way and they had to stop.

Phil, with his years of experience, braked hard and stopped. His mate (who was following) didn't even attempt to stop. He tried to swerve. But this was beyond his skill level, especially when combined with panic. He crashed into Phil and broke his leg.

The mate later explained that he didn't trust his brakes would stop him. According to Phil, this is a common fear with inexperienced riders.

'I run a workshop where I get riders to do an emergency stop at 100 mph,' he said. 'Brakes *work*. Don't be scared of using them!'

> **'LIFE IS SCARY WHEN YOU THINK ABOUT ALL THE THINGS THAT COULD GO WRONG. LIFE IS BRILLIANT WHEN YOU THINK ABOUT ALL THE THINGS THAT COULD GO RIGHT.'**
>
> **Jessica Zahra, long distance adventure rider**

Venting

We can talk about managing anxiety and building confidence, but still some beginners will return from a ride feeling traumatised. The traffic was scary, they messed up, kept stalling, had a too-close encounter with a car …

We can't hold all that emotion and stress in the body. It's not good for us. We need to let it go.

One thing I find useful is venting. Here's the method I use:

- Lie down somewhere quiet and close your eyes. Take a few deep breaths to calm yourself down.

- Focus on the emotion you want to be rid of and picture it as smoke.

- Imagine the smoke getting thicker, filling your body. What colour is the smoke? See the colour really brightly. See the smoke curling and shifting.

- Once your body is full of smoke, it's time to release (vent) it. Imagine there's a chimney on the top of your head. It's old-fashioned, like the whistle on a steam train. There's a hinged lid. If you pull a chain, the lid lifts up.

- So when you're ready, imagine the chain has been pulled and the lid has lifted. Visualise the smoke pouring out, every last bit of it.

Once is usually enough for me, but if I feel there's more to come, I close my eyes and do it again.

Breathe

Taking a few deep breaths *always* helps, especially if you stop to focus on them.

It's definitely worth taking a couple of calming breaths before each manoeuvre in your Mod 1 test. There's no rush to finish. You will have plenty of time.

Flowers to the Rescue

Have you tried Rescue Remedy pastilles? Many women use them to calm nerves before tests. They are very small herbal pastilles, so small that you can slip one between your jaw bone and your cheek so it melts during your test.

Rescue Remedy is also available as a spray or as a liquid. If you need to avoid alcohol, be aware that regular Rescue Remedy contains a tiny amount of it. There is now a dropper version that is alcohol free (and vegan).

Menopause Matters

If you are struggling with anxiety, it might be your hormones. Creeping anxiety is one of the main problems the menopause brings. Suddenly things you used to do with ease fill you with an overwhelming sense of dread.

The actress Jackie Clune has spoken about developing stage fright after decades of performing. She was in the West End, playing the lead in *Mamma Mia!* when it began. She would be standing in the wings, waiting to go on, shaking with fear. It had never been a problem in the past.

A woman told me she had stopped horse riding in her forties because of anxiety, yet she had ridden since childhood.

One of my friends described a moment in her garage when she found she was unable to get on her beloved bike. She went into complete meltdown, feeling she simply couldn't ride it. This is someone who had ridden motorcycles for twenty years. As soon as she started HRT, her confidence returned.

I have heard this kind of story so many times at women's meets. When a group of menopausal women bikers get together, the conversation always gets lively when anxiety and HRT are mentioned. Always there will be someone who has been struggling with a drop in confidence. She isn't riding as far as she used to, or she isn't finding it as enjoyable as it was.

Menopause can make you feel very isolated. There's a dreadful uncertainty to it. So many questions can fill your head. If you're one of the ones who usually gets on with things, it can be deeply distressing to find yourself behaving so weakly. Nothing works. You tell yourself to snap out of it, but you can't.

It's cruelly ironic that for many women, the age when they want to embrace freedom coincides with the hormonal rollercoaster of menopause.

The good news is that the sisterhood is out there. If you are feeling anxious, joining a women's group might give you exactly the reassurance and support you need. Try it!

When A Ride Spirals Down

While we're on the subject of hormones, have you ever had a ride that started off badly and never improved? So you ended up wondering: *What the hell is wrong with me today?*

You might been suffering from the lasting effect of a hormone rush.

Motorcycling is a chemical rollercoaster. Your body releases a cocktail of hormones as you ride. Some are wonderful:

Oxytocin is the bonding hormone. If this one is coursing through your veins, you will be feeling in love with your bike.

Dopamine is the reward hormone. When you are first learning, you get big hits of this one all the time. Did a junction well? *Boom!* Handled a hill start? *Boom!* This is why learning feels so pleasurable.

Serotonin is the happiness hormone. If you're enjoying the ride, this one will be flowing.

Endorphins relieve stress and pain and bring a feeling of euphoria. If you're riding your bike and feeling wild and free, that's the work of endorphins.

But some hormones are double-edged. They are the 'fight or flight' hormones.

Adrenaline is released when your body is facing something exciting, dangerous, stressful or threatening. It helps your body react faster by speeding up your heart to pump more blood to your brain and muscles. This happens so fast, it comes as that adrenaline 'rush' every biker knows and loves.

Cortisol is the stress hormone. Like adrenaline, it is released when things get threatening. So if you're out riding and a car suddenly comes out of nowhere and nearly side-wipes you - *boom!* You'll instantly take a hit of this.

Your adrenaline and cortisol levels will begin to drop once the threat has passed, but it can take an *hour* for them to return to normal. And while they are still raised, you can feel the effects:

- A sense of breathlessness
- Jittery muscles, shaking or trembling
- Rapid heartbeat
- A feeling of anxiety
- Difficulty concentrating

So you can see how one moment of drama can affect your ongoing ride.

I became aware of the connection when I did my European trip. On the first night, my friend and I stayed in the middle of Rouen, a very busy city. The next morning began with two incredibly steep ramps in an underground car park. Next came fifteen minutes of rush hour traffic, followed by a fast ride on an expressway. Then we were out into the French countryside. It was gorgeous, I should have been as happy as a lark. But I wasn't.

We passed through a village and I messed up every junction. It was like I had completely forgotten how to stop. I was grabbing the front brake, making the bike lurch, but couldn't stop doing it. I felt like I was going to drop the bike, and that just added to the mounting sense of panic.

Then my friend pulled into a cafe car park. I followed and found it was *gravel*. I stopped dead and had a complete meltdown, refusing to go any further. My friend had to park the bike for me.

Even when I got into the cafe, it continued. I couldn't eat or drink. My head was spinning like a washing machine. *You can't do it… Day 2 and look at you… Why did you ever think you could do it…* On and on and on!

This was all adrenaline at work. My body was swimming in the stuff. It had worked brilliantly, getting me out of Rouen. But now, as I came down from the rush, my hands weren't working properly and my brain was wrecked. I had to carry on riding, but the whole morning passed before I started to feel any sense of ease or pleasure.

As a new rider, you will get heart-in-the-mouth moments. The adrenaline-cortisol cocktail will hit your blood stream whether you want it or not. It's the body's way of keeping you safe, after all.

Having some understanding of what's happening will help. It's not you, and it will pass in an hour or so.

In the meantime, deep breathing can help, along with a bit of conscious calming. Take a cafe break, but avoid caffeine. Try a herbal tea instead. Camomile is especially calming.

'Help! I go too slow...'

'You can't go fast on a slow bend'

Simon Hayes, Motorcycle Riders Hub

Learners go slow - fact! You can only go as fast as your brain will allow you to go.

When you slow down, your brain is buying time. It is juggling information to find a safe solution to the problem in hand. If it needs time to manage that, it will send a message to your hand and hey presto, you'll come off the throttle.

It's reassuring to know your brain is looking after you, but it does nothing to help your confidence when you see a stream of cars behind you.

"I don't want to hold everyone up…"

Women are very good at putting others first. We don't want to be a bother, get in the way, ruin the enjoyment of others. If we feel we're slow, we might not join group rides.

Riding solo, we don't want to hear those honked horns, or see those angry expressions as impatient drivers blast past us.

So we don't go.

We need to think differently about speed.

Here are a couple of things that might help:

Professional racers slow down on bends

> → On the Isle of Man TT circuit, there's a section called the Sulby Straight. In 2015, James Hillier clocked a record 207

mph here on a Kawasaki Ninja H2R.

→ There is also a bend at Governor's Bridge. The lowest speed clocked here is 18 mph.

18 mph! A pro racer!

You're not being a wuss when you slow down for bends. You are no different to a TT racer. You are working within physical laws (angles, momentum, weight) and limits (how fast your brain can make the calculation)

A fast rider is not necessarily a good rider.

→ Some people are so keen to get out on the road, they do as little training as possible. Once they are legal and on the road, their main aim (as the police will tell you) is to get fast, especially on the bends.

→ Someone with poor training can get faster and faster, but they will still be a poor rider.

→ Someone who takes their time, laying down strong foundations, will get faster in time *and* be a good rider.

→ Which would you rather be?

Therapy: WingWave and NLP

My riding was transformed with one Wingwave session. It's a revolutionary German practice that works with REM (rapid eye movement) to file away triggering thoughts.

I had Wingwave after a few months of having my full licence. I was becoming *so* wary when riding, it was becoming a problem. I was avoiding roads I had happily done on my 125 because they had hill junctions or bad bends. I had taken a tumble on frost over the winter -

that hadn't helped. The road seemed full of hazards and danger. (See **Confidence Going In Reverse**)

It couldn't go on. I was planning a road trip across Europe with a friend. How could I cope with the Pyrenees if I couldn't face a simple hill start?

My therapist friend Deborah suggested Wingwave. It's a type of NLP (see below) The session took an hour and was very simple. Little more than a chat, really. We focussed on memories that were affecting me, like the frost tumble, and she filed them away in another part of my brain. Then she replaced the bad thoughts with good ones. How did I want to feel when I was riding?

I flew home from her house on my bike afterwards. The ride felt totally light and joyous. As I approached Chipping Campden, I suddenly felt the urge to take one of the 'avoided' roads.

It had a very bad hill stop/start junction at the end of it. Before the Wingwave, I would have approached it with my heart in my mouth, panic hammering in my chest. My head would have been full of desperate commands to myself: *do it, just do it, keep going....*

But now the panic was gone. GONE. No word of a lie, I headed for the junction with a sense of happy excitement. The approach was very bumpy - at one point I was bumped out of the saddle. Normally that would have added to the anxiety. Now I laughed. This was fun!

I did the junction perfectly and rode on.

A couple of weeks after the Wingwave, I did that European trip. I faced some real challenges but that heart-hammering, fluttery panic feeling *never* returned. I have not avoided any roads since. Wingwave was nothing short of a miracle for me.

Neuro Linguistic Programming (NLP)

If, like me, you're old enough to remember playing vinyl records, you'll remember that sometimes a record would get stuck in a groove. It would keep playing the same line over and over again. The only solution was to knock the side of the record player. This usually made the stylus jump into a new groove.

Our brains can get stuck in grooves too. Every time we are faced with a certain situation, our brain will react the same way, whether we want it to or not. It can be very limiting.

NLP is the therapeutic equivalent of that knock on the side of the record player. It can move you on, very swiftly.

I can say this with certainty because one of my exes was an NLP practitioner, and he told me about one of his clients, a passionate horse rider who had taken a bad fall and been unable to get on a horse since. She wanted to ride - she would be in her riding gear, standing beside the horse. But then she would be overcome by anxiety and simply couldn't climb into the saddle.

My ex sorted this in a single one-hour session. His client was back in the saddle the very next day.

NLP is a bit like re-programming a computer, which is what your brain is, after all. It's not invasive or deeply revealing. It's more like a structured conversation.

If you're struggling because of a bad biking experience (like a tumble or being knocked off) both of these are well worth considering.

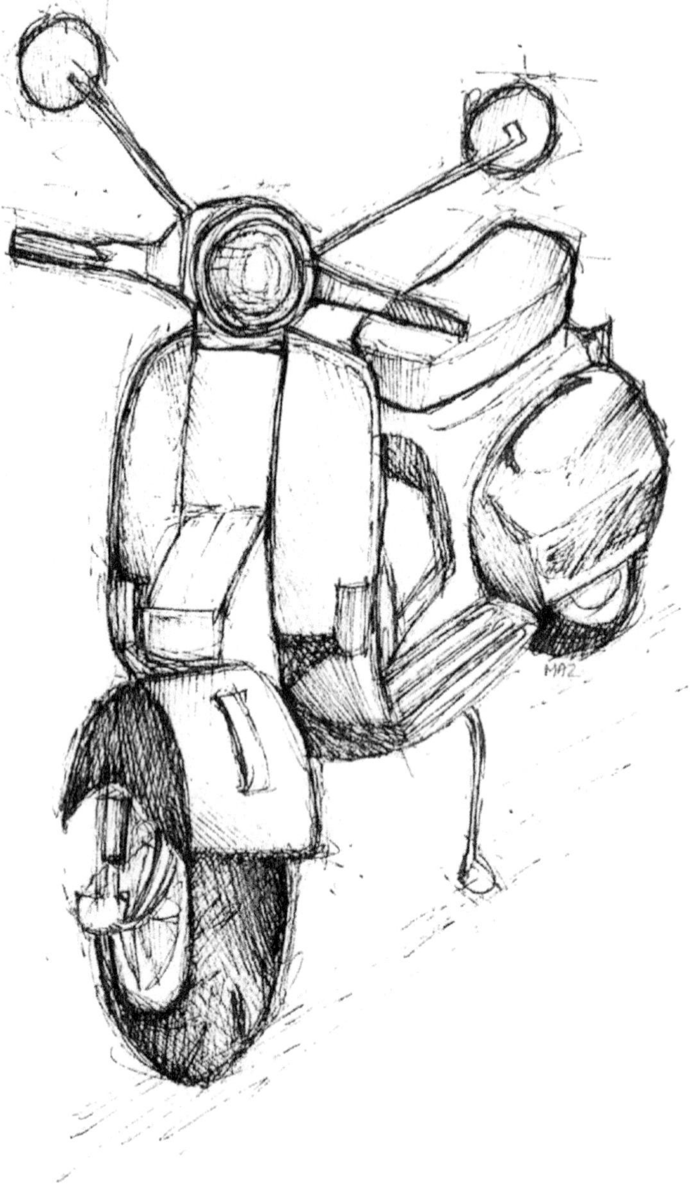
MAZ

PART 10: DROPPING THE BIKE

Every biker drops a bike at some stage in their biking career. It's embarrassing, it can hurt, but it's perfectly normal.

Learners are more prone to it, but it can happen even to seasoned riders. A momentary lapse of concentration, a steep camber at a junction, a gravelly car park - *doomf!* Down you go.

It happens to men and women alike. Yet women seem to worry about it far more than men, especially when they are learning. Often it goes hand-in-hand with a fear of stalling: *'I'm afraid to turn right at junctions in case I stall and drop the bike.'*

When I did my European trip, I was so worried about dropping the bike and breaking a lever, I carried a spare set of clutch/brake levers with me. They came back unused. My riding buddy didn't understand my need to carry them in the first place.

'Why do you think you are going to drop the bike?' he said. 'It never enters my head that I might drop the bike.'

I have heard other women say their male partners have told them the same thing.

For many women, fear of dropping the bike is more the fear they won't be able to pick it up again.

Bikes are bloody heavy. I am always worried about putting my back out, and then I'd have two problems instead of one. But that is me, catastrophising again! There are many videos on YouTube in which tiny women pick up motorcycles the size of motorhomes. They all make it look incredibly easy, and they always say it is down to technique. While this is true, it can still be a real struggle.

I confess, when I dropped my 650, out on my own, I didn't even attempt to try lifting it. I was riding alone, it was a Sunday and I was on a road popular with bikers. 'There will be someone along soon,' I said gaily to a concerned bystander who wanted to help but didn't know how. Sure enough, a big hairy biker came along within a couple of minutes and stopped to help.

So if you ride alone and are worried about not being able to pick your bike up, have faith that someone will help. You are not alone: you are part of a biking family. I have always found other bikers enormously helpful.

But watch the videos too. Learn those techniques. I was lucky - I was on a main road. It would have been a different story if I had been on my own miles from anywhere.

How does it feel to drop a bike?

When you drop a bike, it seems to go in slow motion. That's my experience. There was always a moment when I heard myself say *she's going down,* and then she did.

When you get to this point, don't try to hold the bike up. You've passed the point of saving it. If you try to hold it, you can damage your shoulder muscles, and you *really* don't want that. So let the bike go and focus on getting clear of it. Sometimes this is possible, sometimes not.

Isn't it embarrassing?

Yes, it is embarrassing if you do it on the road, but by-standers and drivers seem to react with horror more than hoots of laughter. I suspect it looks worse than it feels. It's also unexpected, which adds to the drama for onlookers.

If you do it in front of other bikers, they will be sympathetic. They've all been there. They will offer help. Accept it.

What to do next

Take a deep breath and get back on. It's not always easy. You might be winded or bruised. Your body will be awash with stress hormones, so you might feel jittery. You might feel anxious about riding a bike that has just taken a knock.

For all these reasons, ride carefully - but RIDE. Leave the drop behind you. You can't fix it. But learn from it too. There is *always* a reason why the bike dropped - find it. There was a camber you didn't notice … you were looking down at the road instead of up … you were planning to go then had to stop unexpectedly … the revs were too low …. the gear was too high…. Whatever it was, make a mental note to do it better next time.

How often should I drop my bike?

While everyone drops a bike occasionally, it shouldn't be a regular part of your road riding, even when you're a beginner.

If it is, be honest about your bike and your ability to handle it. Is it too tall for you? Too top-heavy?

The times when you drop it… Can you spot a pattern? Does it always happen at a junction? When you are trying to park? When you have to stop on an incline? Go to a car park and practise that manoeuvre.

Some people make dropping the bike sound like a joke. No big deal. But -

- It can hurt. It generally doesn't hurt much, because you are going at such a slow speed, but you can get heavy bruising. A broken wrist is a possibility too.
- You can damage the bike, breaking off levers etc Even if you don't break anything, scratches and dents are almost guaranteed.
- It can wreck your confidence. If you've been doing well in your

training, it can come as a real shock. If you've been struggling, it can add to your growing sense of despair.

It feels like I'm being a gloom and doom merchant here, focussing on all the bad things that can go wrong. But I don't have the money to pay extra garage bills, and an injury is no joke if it stops you working. I want to avoid it.

I realised I was unstable on my 650 at junctions because I was looking down at the road when I came to a stop. Many drops are caused by this. It really unbalances you. You must keep looking up, with your head straight.

I sorted this by consciously fixing my eyes on a target for the last few seconds before I stopped. Sometimes it would be a traffic light or a road sign.

Sometimes it would be something on one of the taller vehicles in the queue ahead of me, like the tail light on the roof of a van.

In my head I would be saying: *Look at the light, look at the light, look at the light.* Over and over again. Doing this made me 100% present with my head up. I still do it now if I'm having a bit of a wobbly day. I have never dropped the bike since I started doing this.

PART 11: MIND YOUR LANGUAGE

It's only a 125....

'He's only a baby. But I hope to have a proper child one day.'

Women are prone to using limiting language. We reduce ourselves and our achievements, shrug off compliments and justify our actions all the time.

We apologise endlessly.

I was at a bike festival, in a marquee, listening to adventure biker Steph Jeavons. It was very informal, with everyone sitting on hay bales. There was no roving microphone when it was time for the audience to ask questions.

A few men asked questions then a woman raised her hand. Steph acknowledged her and the woman said: 'I'm sorry, you probably can't hear me but ...'

The truth was, she was no quieter than any of the men, yet none of them had felt the need to apologise. Ironically, Steph had just been talking about how women speak on the phone when they call to enquire about her off-road courses.

'They say things like 'I don't know if I'll be fast enough' or 'I don't want to hold anyone up,' she told us. 'The men *never* say things like that.'

I came out with the *It's only a 125 line* when I first took my CB125F to Broadway in the Cotswolds. It was my first long trip - thirty minutes! On my own! I felt dizzy with pride as I parked her in a motorcycle bay alongside half a dozen BMWs the size of buffaloes.

When I returned from my celebratory tea break, the owners of these bikes were there, gearing up. They were all men in their sixties and very friendly. Despite my L plates, they greeted me as a fellow biker, and one of them said how smart-looking my bike was.

I smiled. 'It's only a 125.'

'A 125 is a motorbike,' he said. 'Nothing more to say. And let me tell you, *that* is harder to ride than this.' He indicated his own bike. 'Look at the width of my tyres compared to yours. This sits on the road, whereas yours gets blown all over the place in the wind, yes? If you can handle that, you're doing well. I think every biker, no matter how big their bike, should get on a 125 once a year, to remind themselves how it feels. It is raw and real, the closest to true biking you can get, and it's why we all got involved in the first place.'

There's nothing small about a 125. I rode my 125 all around the Cotswolds in my first summer of biking and loved every minute. I did my DAS with a man who had done a full-on road trip to Scotland on his 125, Birmingham to the Orkneys, with a tent and all his gear strapped onto the back. Still with L plates, so back roads all the way.

'You can go anywhere with a 125,' he said. 'It took me a bit more time, but I never broke down. Great adventure!'

Own your achievements. Be proud of your bike, L plates and all. Accept compliments with a smile. You're doing great - believe it.

Listen to Yourself

Negative language isn't helpful. Whether you are talking to yourself or to others, turn those negatives into something more positive.

Try saying some of these and see the difference it makes.

Negative	Positive
I am too slow	I am not fast
I am rubbish on bends	I am still learning how best to corner
I'm such a wuss	I am naturally cautious
I failed	I wasn't successful this time
I don't think I will ever be able to…	It's taking me a bit longer than some people, but …
That junction is a nightmare	That junction needs more practice
It was a disaster	It was very revealing, because I saw …

Re-word your life!

Shut The F**k Up!

Hands up if you've ever shouted, swore or yelled in your helmet? I have, countless times. I still do on occasion, if I'm being honest. It might release tension, but according to the experts, there's a much better alternative.

Imagine you are out riding and the road suddenly becomes challenging. Tractors have covered it with mud or there's an incredibly steep hill you weren't expecting. It's way beyond your confidence level.

Your natural response might be to swear repeatedly and hold on for dear life till it's over, but the off-road experts (who deal with far worse for pleasure) say the better response is to take a deep breath and talk yourself through the process. *'Ease off the throttle, change down to third, down to second…'*

Don't be a victim - take control.

May All Your Mantras Be Good Ones

If you're anything like me, you will have a head full of mantras as you learn to ride. Mantras - those little sayings you repeat to yourself to help you focus and do things right. They might be things your trainer has given you, like *Turn, look, aim,* or they might be things you have come up with yourself.

I used a host of them in my Mod 1. *Look at the lorries… look at the car park… look at the blue bin… look at the fence* was my figure of eight sequence. It kept me present and pointing the bike exactly where it needed to go.

So they can work brilliantly well, but it is really important that they are *positive* ones, otherwise they can work against you. It's all to do with how the brain works.

If I say to you now: *Don't think about an elephant* what instantly comes into your mind? Yep. Your brain is like a search engine. It ignores the nuances of 'do and don't' and instead grabs hold of 'elephant,' whizzes through its memory banks and pops up the image in your head. It is being helpful, bless it.

Except it hasn't helped at all. I wanted you not to think about an elephant.

It is the same with mantras.

I was horrified on the morning of my test when my instructor Mike (trying to be helpful) said to me in my earpiece: *'On the swerve manoeuvre, don't look at the outside blue cone.'*

No!!!

To be fair, the full advice was *'Don't look at the outside blue cone because then you will steer towards it. Focus on the inside blue cone and you will be fine.'* But the image was already planted. And he had said it himself: *because then you will steer towards it.*

Thankfully I was aware of all this, so as I accelerated towards the manoeuvre, I was almost shouting *Look at the INSIDE cone, the INSIDE cone, the INSIDE cone* and my brain heard me, focussed my eyes in the right place and the bike followed.

I truly believe it's worth knowing this. I'm not making it up! This is proven neuroscience. Make sure all your mantras are positive.

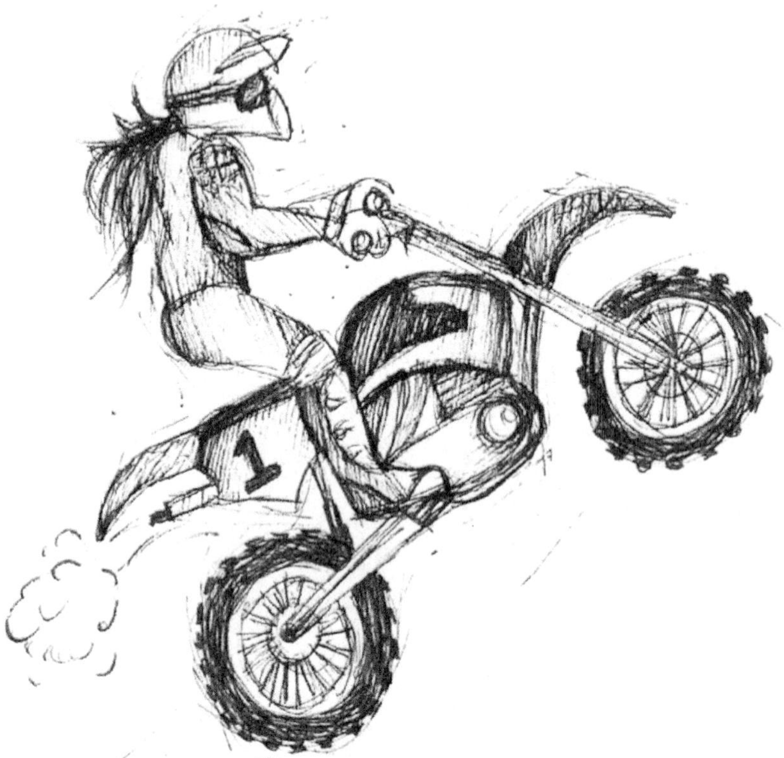

PART 12:
MOVING UP TO A BIG BIKE

'Should I start DAS and get a full licence?'

I think you will know the answer to this question when the time comes. I certainly did.

Much as I had loved my 125, I knew I was ready to move on. For me, it was mostly about safety. I'd had a few scary moments on busy dual carriageways, trying to cross lanes to do a right turn. With cars hurtling up behind me, I didn't have the power to accelerate into spaces. Frantically I would look over my shoulder, praying someone would let me in. Often they didn't.

Also I was itching to do a long road trip. I know some women have travelled around the UK on 125s, but I struggled on hills and overtaking was an impossibility. I also wanted the option of taking the motorway.

You'll have your own reason, whether it's the dream of a particular bike or a desire to ride with friends who are on bigger machines.

Is it easier to ride a big bike than a 125?

It *is* easier to ride a big bike, but that doesn't mean it is easy. It is not the miracle cure some women seem to suggest. You need to be safe and competent on a 125 before stepping up.

This is true:

- Bigger bikes sit on the road (or car park) better. Their weight makes them more stable.

- They are smoother at low speed in the low gears. Their engines 'tick over' better, so they are less likely to stall when doing slow manoeuvres.

- Their wider tyres make it easier to ride on bad road surfaces, especially those ones that seem to have tram lines in them.

- They feel more stable in the wind (though they can still get thrown all over the place)

- The extra power brings confidence. You can accelerate into spaces and out of trouble. You can overtake safely.

But you will also find this to be true:

- They are *much* heavier to manually handle. To this day, I hate the feeling of dropping a heavy bike down onto its side stand when the camber is a bit steep.

- They are much more powerful. Some women find the torque scary to begin with. Torque is the pulling power of a bike. The 'oomph.' 125s are not torquey! You usually have to kick them hard to make them go. I regularly rode mine with the throttle fully turned. A big bike feels nothing like that. You hold the throttle very gently but still, with the slightest movement, the bike comes alive and feels like it wants to roar away with you. It can take a little time to get used to, if you're not a confident rider.

- They are less 'forgiving' than 125s. They are much more sensitive. If you grab for the front brake on a 125, you'll have a dodgy stop. Do it on a 650 and chances are, you'll be down.

Losing the L plates

Blog Post, September 2021

I was very interested to see what difference it made once I was out on a big bike with no L plates. Had people been making allowances for me as a learner?

I had been constantly overtaken on my 125, especially turning left at roundabouts when drivers would take advantage of my dropped speed to grab a quick overtake. Dominating the lane made no difference - they would still do it, even if it meant dangerously squeezing me.

But I was also aware drivers had been giving me space and time at junctions. They wouldn't pull up too close. They didn't beep me if I stalled. They frequently slowed the traffic and waved me across when I was turning right across a busy road. I had never felt especially pressured by someone behind me.

I would lose all these benefits along with the L plates. Now I would be expected to ride with a degree of competence I wouldn't always have.

As it turned out, the dangerous overtaking stopped. I was able to accelerate faster at the roundabouts and the bigger bike dominated the lane more easily. I think people assume a bike will speed away at lights so don't even try to pressure them.

I haven't had problems with anyone trying to race me, even on motorways. Maybe I would be raced more if I had a racing bike? I can't say.

Equally I can't say what difference being female makes, if any. I have pink flashes on my jacket and blonde hair poking from beneath my helmet, so I am unmistakably a girl. I sometimes felt, as a learner, people gave me an even greater berth because I was a woman. If that was true, I really didn't mind. As I wobbled my way though some very tricky junctions, I felt they were wise to stay well back!

The Theory Test

You will need to pass this before you can take your Mods. It consists of a series of multiple choice questions and hazard awareness videos.

You do it in a room at a test centre. It all feels very top secret. You have to put your bag in a locker and it is very quiet. The room is full of individual booths, each with a computer screen. You wear headphones.

Do I need to study for the test?

You should read The Highway Code. Even if there was no theory test, you should read The Highway Code. It is there to protect you, both physically and legally. The information it contains will save you from getting tickets, warn you of hazards, give you greater awareness of road conditions and help you if you end up in an argument with a driver.

The failure rate is high, at nearly 50%. It may be multiple choice but that doesn't make it easy. I studied for hours (I'm that kind of person) and still had questions in my test I had never seen before.

So I would say yes, do a bit of studying, because failing never feels good. The best way of studying is with an app. It is worth paying a little more and getting one with hazard videos because they are usually the reason people fail.

The hazard videos work like this:

- You watch a clip, shown from the point of view of a driver/rider (The hazard videos are the same whether you are sitting a car theory test or a motorcycle one.)

- You have to look for developing hazards. Each clip will contain one hazard. Once you spot the hazard developing, you click the mouse and score points. Five is the maximum you can score per clip.

Sounds easy, yes?

It is fairly easy if you're a seventeen year-old learning to drive. That is who the test is designed for.

With respect to seventeen year-olds, they generally have low road awareness. They are inexperienced drivers. Whereas many women who begin biking are drivers with years of experience behind them.

There is a 'window,' a point at which the points begin and finish. They count down, 5-4-3-2-1, so if you click immediately you can score 5 but if you're slow, you can miss out altogether.

For drivers, the problem is not clicking too late, it's clicking too soon. As a driver, you will almost certainly spot the hazard before the scoring window opens. So you click - and score nothing.

The only way to improve, if you are clicking too early, is to practise with the videos. You must learn to play the game well. My app was brilliant. Once I had done a clip, I was able to see my score and then replay the clip with the window showing. This instantly showed me exact point at which the countdown had begun.

Why can't you just click repeatedly? Make sure you hit the window?

Wouldn't that be easy! Sadly, if you click too many times, your score will be discounted. You will score nothing for that clip.

Most people seem to agree that the best method is to double-click. You click when you feel it's right - wait a second - and then click again. This gives you a better chance of scoring if you were a bit early.

Don't get too hung up about over-clicking. If you see a hazard and do your double-click then realise that probably wasn't the hazard, you can do another double-click when the 'proper' one comes along. It's just repeated clicking that scores nothing.

If you fail the test, you sit it again. It's no big deal.

Do your theory as soon as you start thinking about DAS. Get it out of the way, then you can book training with no fear of set-backs.

Starting DAS

No two riders have the same journey. Some riders sail through DAS in a few days while others find they are right back to struggling again. If you find it harder than you were expecting, hang on in there. It will get easier in time. Your body just needs a little longer to adapt.

DAS trains you for two tests. Mod 1 takes place on a special test site and involves certain slow manoeuvres including an emergency stop, a swerve, a figure of eight and a u-turn.

Once you have passed Mod 1, you progress to Mod 2. Most people feel this is the easier test. It is on-road riding with an examiner riding behind you.

When you pass Mod 2, you gain your full licence.

'Should I do DAS intensively over a few days or take it slowly?'

This is a matter of preference. I did it slowly, over a matter of weeks, because that suited my learning style. I don't like to feel over-loaded by information. I like to take what I've learned and practise on my own to embed it.

I am very much a 'list ticker.' I liked getting my Mod 1 done before turning my attention to Mod 2. One thing at a time, that's me! I didn't want to feel rushed.

On the other hand, you could argue that taking it slowly gives you time to over-think. I was going well with my u-turns then started to go backwards. This made me panic. I was practising for hours, trying this method, that method. My confidence was eroding, day by day.

If I had been on an intensive, I would simply have got on with it. It a no-nonsense approach.

Whatever route you choose, you need to keep the momentum of learning going. This is why most people start learning in the spring. Not only does it give you something to look forward to - a whole summer on your new bike - it removes any worry about having to train or test in bad weather. Some women fail their Mods repeatedly, and it can take time to get a new test date.

Women do train and pass their Mods in the winter. A Mod 1 test site has a special surface that makes it safe to do emergency stops even in the rain. But tests (and lessons) will be cancelled if conditions get too bad.

I think if you're confident of passing, an intensive course is fine any time of the year. If you want the slower approach, spring is better.

Don't compare yourself to others

Once you start training for your Mods, you might find yourself in the company of more experienced riders. Don't let this put you off. They might not be as skilful as you think.

Many men return to biking after decades away. The kids have gone and they're hungry for the road again.

I met several such guys during my DAS. They had all ridden extensively in the past and all knew exactly what bike they would buy once they had passed.

They were nice, but I confess I found them intimidating to begin with. They climbed onto the training bikes so confidently. They knew what they were doing.

That was what I told myself. In truth, it was a different story. When I chatted to them over lunch, one to one, I found they had the same confidence issues as the rest of us. They were acutely aware of their rustiness. Most had no formal training. It wasn't the way when they were younger. They had climbed on the bike and ridden.

William was in his fifties. He had a beautiful leather jacket, gorgeous boots and a brand-new Indian Scout in his garage, waiting for him to pass.

He seemed very confident and capable. His test was later that week. This was his one and only lesson. A refresher.

We went with Laura to the test site to do a few circuits. William was very confident. But even I could see his stopping was questionable. You have to stop *under control,* that's what the test rules say. William's style might be best described as *over-exuberant.*

Still I believed he would pass. He was so confident! But he didn't. He failed his Mod 1. He needed more time to shake off those bad habits.

I took my Mod 1 two days after him and passed.

'Can I use my own bike to do my Mods?' *

Theoretically yes, as long as it meets the test requirements concerning engine size. But getting insurance will be a problem because you're trying to insure a bike you're not legally qualified to ride. You can get your partner to ride the bike to the test centre, or take it on a trailer, but to be honest, nearly everyone uses a training school bike. They have the proper insurance and it's just so much simpler.

* I am talking about the A and A2 licences here. You can do the A1 licence tests on your own 125. People who do this are called *privateers* because they (generally) aren't there with an instructor.

PART 13:
PREPARING FOR THE MODS

You've had your training, your test date is approaching - fast. What can you do to calm those butterflies?

Here are some positive suggestions.

Stay away from social media

If you're the anxious type, it can be very tempting to start posting things like

Ladies, I have my Mod 1 in two days time and am freaking out already!! Any advice pleeeeeze??

Yes, you will get advice and lots of 'You'll smash it!' messages from people who have no knowledge of your riding ability. They will all be kindly meant, and maybe they will buoy you up and help you feel less alone.

But in truth, all a panic-post does is reveal how little self-confidence you have. *That* is what you need to work on.

Picture it like a lake. If you make a panic-post, every reply is like a pebble thrown into the water. Splash, splash, ripple, ripple. When what you *really* need is for the lake to be smooth and quiet.

You've had your lessons. You know what you have to do. Now you need to sit with yourself and start believing you can do it.

Try not to dwell on it. You will only start to over-think and catastrophise. It's only a test. You're not having surgery. Keep a sense of proportion.

All this is easier said than done, I know. The best way to stop yourself over-thinking is to put that brain activity to better use. If you really must do something, consider writing a Benefits List. This will help boost your positive thinking.

Make a Benefits List

Make a list of the benefits of passing your Mod 1. Anything you can think of. It's for your eyes only, so be honest. This is not a time to be thinking *Does that make me vain/ shallow/ arrogant / a pleaser/ whatever.* If posting an 'I did it!!' photo on Facebook would make you happy-dance round the kitchen, list it. List whatever works for you. This was my list:

BENEFITS LIST

1. I can tell Katrice I've passed. She will be so proud of me.
2. I can post a photo on Facebook and loads of people will like it.
3. I will be one step closer to Mod 2.
4. I will never have to do another 'perfect' u-turn. If I want to put my foot down, I can!
5. I will never have to ride to Garrett's Green ever again!! (My Mod 1 test centre was in a very busy part of Birmingham. Riding there always felt like stepping into a video game, with endless hazards and pressure.)
6. I will not have to spend any more money on Mod 1 training.

Some of you might be thinking *but what if I do this and don't pass? Won't it make me feel worse? I will have to tell (name) I failed and ...*

This is future thinking. Worrying about something that hasn't even happened. It is a complete waste of time and energy. If it happens, it happens. Deal with it then, not now.

We get what we focus on. You remember the inside/outside blue cone? (**May All Your Mantras Be Good Ones**) Focus on failing and you increase your chances of doing it. As part of their training, athletes visualise the entire race, from the bang of the starting pistol to crossing the winning line. They run this movie over and over in their heads until it is automatic and then, on the day, the brain thinks it's business as usual and delivers.

Do they visualise tripping as they leave the blocks? Or hitting the first hurdle? Being overtaken in the final ten metres?

No. They visualise a perfect, winning race.

They might be out-run on the day. You might hit a cone. It happens. We are human. But that doesn't mean the process is flawed. Use it.

Put the Bubbly in the Fridge

I was so determined to behave as if I had already passed, I bought a celebratory Thank You card and present for Laura and took them with me to my Mod 1 test. Inside the card I wrote 'Yippee!! We did it! Thank you so much x' The present bag included a small bottle of bubbly and chocolates.

I also bought a bottle of bubbly for myself and put it in the fridge on the morning of my test. I told myself 'You are going to be celebrating tonight, lady!' And that proved true.

Buy yourself a bottle of something nice and put it in the fridge!

What are you wearing?

This is not the time to be wearing new gloves or boots. If these things aren't worn in, they can seriously affect your confidence and your handling of the bike. New boots can make you repeatedly go into neutral; new gloves can make you rev the engine.

Do you dip your shoulder to go into manoeuvres, like the U-turn? You might find a sports bra is better than a regular one - the straps won't slip down. This might sound like a trivial thing, but a slipped strap is a distraction that can escalate into a worry if you are the anxious type.

It was a JOKE - wasn't it?

I remember a woman on Facebook who had failed her Mod 1 twice and was heading for her third attempt. What struck me about her posts was the photos and memes she was choosing to use. They were all fear images. Yes, they were jokey ones: wide-eyed cats and dogs, or memes taken from horror movies, showing people trembling in fear. But your brain believes what you tell it. If you choose negative, fearful images, even in jest, you are warning it to be alert. *There is danger in this situation. Be ready.*

On test day your brain *will* be ready. It will pump you full of stress hormones to prepare you for a battle. When actually what you need is the opposite, to enter the site feeling calm and happy.

Every life coach will tell you: focus on the positive. Fill your head with *successful* images. Picture yourself where you want to be, not where you are now.

Buy a pin board and fill it with images of the new, successful biker you. Bikes, clothes, fields full of sunflowers - make it bright. Ride into sunshine, not rain clouds.

Don't Pile On the Pressure

A test is stressy enough without adding to the pressure. I was fine with my Mod 1 but became very stressed about my Mod 2. Looking back now, I can see that none of it was to do with my riding ability. It was all to do with externals: time, money, other people's expectations of me.

It's easier said than done, but you need to let external pressures go. Whatever happens, happens. Deal with the fallout then.

If you fail your test, you'll book a new date and try again.

The world won't end. You won't lose your job. The sun will still shine every morning, even if it's hidden by clouds.

No one will die.

It's just a test.

On the Day

I found the real Mod 1 test easier than the practice circuits. I know that sounds crazy, but it's true. It was quieter, calmer. No one was watching. No instructor was talking in my ear. There was no striving to get it right. In a strange way, it seemed too late for that. It felt more like what will be, will be.

There are a few reassuring things I'd like to share with you.

1. It is a remarkably short test. You finish before you know it.

2. The manoeuvres are over much sooner than in training. When you're learning, your instructor will make you go round and round and round the figure of eight. Six times? Seven? Eight? On the test it will likely be *twice*.

3. You can ask questions if you are unsure where you need to go. You will not pick up points for asking.

4. There is no rush. You have thirty minutes to complete the test. If you need to stop and breathe, you can.

Eat a banana

Better still, eat two. It's not a myth - bananas can reduce anxiety. They are natural beta-blockers, bringing down both your heart rate and blood pressure. They are rich in potassium too, and your potassium level will drop if you are stressed. Potassium is a vital mineral - it normalises your heartbeat and helps send oxygen to the brain.

Many women swear that eating a banana half an hour before their test helped them pass.

Don't forget to pack your Rescue Remedy pastilles too (See **Flowers to the Rescue**)

'Help! I failed my Mod 1…'

'I am so annoyed with myself! I rode PERFECTLY to the test centre then my nerves got the better of me and my foot went down…'

If you failed, you will know why. You kicked a cone, put your foot down, failed to reach the minimum speed or whatever.

But *why* did you do that? Was it nerves or was it something else? It's worth reflecting until you find an answer that feels right to you. Then you can think about sorting it, ready for your next attempt.

Many women fail simply because they're not test-ready. Some schools will try to push you through and then, when you fail, they'll quote a figure at you.

'It's not unusual to fail. The pass rate is only 64%, you know.'

They are simply covering their backs. My school has a first-time pass rate of 98%. They don't put anyone forward for a test until they are test-ready.

Knowing you are truly test-ready brings confidence.

MOD 2: Let's Do It All Again

The Mod 2 test is an on-road test. It begins with the examiner checking your eyesight (they ask you to read a number plate at the legal distance) Then you are asked a few 'show and tell' questions about the bike. Your school will coach you for these questions.

Then you go out on the road with them. Just like in your lessons, you will be connected to the examiner via a headset. They won't make any comments. They will simply give instructions.

One thing that is different to your training is how far back the examiner stays. They are much further back than you expect them to be, almost out of sight. Don't worry about them. Concentrate on riding your ride.

The on-road loop takes about thirty-five minutes and doesn't include an emergency stop. The 'manoeuvres' include a hill start and pulling up behind a parked vehicle then riding off again. My test seemed to include a great deal of pulling over/ pulling off, and I scored two faults on it. This makes me wonder whether my examiner added in an extra couple to see whether I could do them with greater control than I first demonstrated. Clearly the answer was no!

Is it important to know the test route?

It's impossible to predict the test route because the examiners use many routes. I spent a huge amount of time riding around my local test area before my Mod 2, and practised all the known routes my school showed me, but still there were roads on my test I hadn't been down before.

Does it help if you know the area?

This really depends on what kind of person you are. I gained confidence from knowing the test area because I knew where the hazards were. Some of the road surfaces were bad, some of the roads were very steep, some of the exits from the dual carriage had very tight bends… I liked being able to practise, over and over. There was also a buses-only road that I went down during a lesson, despite my instructor being right behind me! I was so glad I did that *before* my test. Sure enough, I came to that exact stretch of road on my test. It would have been a fail if I'd gone down it then.

I have heard some women say they preferred to do their test in an area they *didn't* know, because it made them more alert. Less complacent. As riders, we are always told to ride the road we are seeing, not the road we think we know. If we are very familiar with an area, it's easy to fall into the trap of assuming things will be the same as usual. *No one ever comes out of that alley way… These lights stay green for a long time…*

I am definitely more focussed when I'm in an unfamiliar area.

Incidentally, you won't fail if you go the wrong way (unless you head the wrong way up a one-way street, obviously!) It is the examiner's job to get you back to the test centre, not yours.

What I did to prepare for my Mod 2

As with Mod 1, I focussed all my attention on thinking positively.

I…

- Wrote another Benefits List

- Did a 'best possible outcome' visualisation

- Bought a little bottle of pink prosecco and put it in the fridge the night before my test, ready for a celebratory drink.

- Coloured and curled my hair, so I would look decent in all those 'I PASSED' photos I was going to be posting.

- Packed a thank you present in my bag for my trainer, Laura

- Went on Autotrader to find the bike I would buy in the afternoon, having passed the test in the morning. Sent 'tell me more' enquiries to three of the dealers with possible bikes. Looked at insurance quotes.

- Pulled my lucky tee shirt out of the laundry basket, the one I'd worn for my Mod 1. The one with the logo that said Fairytale Ending, because that was what was coming.

- Made a list of Things to Bear In Mind for the next day. Anything positive I could think of went on it:

THINGS TO BEAR IN MIND

1. I am absolutely test ready.
2. The weather forecast is dry and sunny.
3. It is at 10.15 - I will miss the school run.
4. Laura is taking me.
5. I will not have to ride around the back streets of Redditch ever again (seven Hells, some of those streets are STEEP!!)

Tips for Mod 2

Chew gum

Chewing gum can help with nerves if you're the jittery type. The saliva it produces is a bonus too, stopping your mouth from getting dry.

Alternatively, suck a Rescue Remedy pastille (see **Flowers to the Rescue**)

Talk your way around

Your examiner won't be able to hear you - the headset you're given doesn't have a microphone. So you can talk aloud the whole way around. Do a running commentary to help you keep 100% focussed:

'I'm in third gear, twenty five miles an hour, car coming out of junction on the left, another behind him, mirror, drop down to second...'

Ride With A Friend

I've heard many women say they defused the tension by imagining they were simply out for a social ride with their friend, not on a test. This is easy to imagine because the examiner stays a long way back. It feels more like riding alone, to be honest. It's nowhere near as intense as a driving test with the examiner sitting in the car next to you!

My #1 Tip

Unfortunate things can happen on your test. You can make mistakes, ride messier than usual because of nerves, feel you're failing. But remember this:

> WHATEVER HAPPENS, KEEP GOING

If you made a mistake, maybe they didn't see it.

Maybe they did see it but it's only a fault.

Maybe they saw it and they *didn't* give it a fault.

You are allowed ten minor faults before you fail.

The examiner will cut you some slack. They know you're nervous. You do not need to be perfect, you simply need to be safe and smooth. What is important is the impression the examiner is getting.

My examiner said to me, 'I thought you were a very confident rider.' I was amazed at this. I had done what I thought was a *very* ragged ride, not helped by a broken mirror (see **My Mod 2**) I returned to the test centre convinced I had failed.

But I *had* put on the gas when it was possible, and I'd coped with everything that came my way. I had got on with it. So I suppose I was 'confident.'

My #2 Tip

This one is simple: GET ON WITH IT

Many women fail because they are too slow or ride over-cautiously. At least, that is what the examiner tells them. The woman usually feels differently. I have read many posts online where women have been indignant about it. They felt they rode confidently. They were simply riding safely.

As someone who is often at the high end of the *better-be-on-the-safe-side* spectrum, I can totally sympathise. It's a bummer of a reason to fail.

When I was doing my DAS, I remember my trainer Laura repeatedly urging me to get up to speed, especially when exiting junctions.

'Get on with it,' she'd say.

Looking back now, I am sure she was telling me this because

- a. It's safer. Junctions are the #1 place for accidents - so why are you hanging around?
- b. Riding slow pisses drivers off and encourages them to overtake.
- c. It's what examiners want.

On your Mod 2, you must get up to speed and ride at the national limit. I have seen women fail for riding at 20 mph in a 30 mph zone. They didn't respond when the transition from one to the other came. Laura was *really* hot on this. Look for the change and respond - instantly.

It's no good doing a perfect ride if it's too slow. Even if it's wet, get on with it. Trust your tyres - they are designed to be ridden in rain. If you need to go to fifty, go to fifty.

Tests are all about ticking boxes. Give them what they want to see.

Remember...

For most women, Mod 2 is straightforward with no real problems.

Nearly everyone feels it is easier than Mod 1 because there is far less pressure.

Many women enjoy it! It feels like a regular ride because the examiner is so far back and doesn't say much.

Most examiners are really nice. Mine definitely was.

It's not the end of the world if you fail. You simply take it again, as soon as you can. Next time you will feel more confident - you will have the experience of having done one before.

You've got this!

PART 14:
BUYING A BIG GIRL BIKE

CONGRATULATIONS! You've done it! You smashed your Mod 2 and now it's time for your first big bike. What should you buy? What's the best bike for you? That's easy...

THE BEST BIKE FOR YOU IS THE BIKE THAT MAKES YOU FEEL CONFIDENT

You need a bike you're itching to ride. You look out of the window at it and sigh longingly. You keep slipping into the garage to stroke it.

You should feel in your heart that you made the right decision when you bought this bike. Any bike is going to feel unfamiliar in the beginning but it shouldn't scare you every time you climb on.

'But I don't know anything about bikes. Where should I start?'

There are so many bikes to choose from, it can seem overwhelming, right? The good news is, it's really easy to start narrowing down the field.

There are only a few basic styles: a cruiser, a racer, a retro classic, a naked roadster or a tourer/adventure bike.

Think about what you want to do with your new bike. If you don't want to go touring or off-roading, you can instantly strike that category off the list (for your first bike at least.) Are you keen to do track days? A cruiser probably isn't the bike for you.

What is important to you? Looks? Comfort? Speed? Power? Low weight? Think about these things. Budget will come into it too.

Do you regularly want to carry a lot of things? A top box is perfect for that but it would completely ruin the look of a bobber. Do you want decent-sized panniers? Some bikes can only accommodate very small ones.

Your body shape will make a difference. If you're short, you might feel more confident on a bike you can flat foot, like a cruiser. If you have a bad back, you might find a racer uncomfortable.

Before you know it, you will have reduced the choice down to just a couple of categories.

Take a look online then find some local biker dealerships to visit. You need to start sitting on bikes - it's the best way to begin.

There are three ways of sitting: leaning forward, leaning back or sitting upright. One you start sitting on bikes, you will know instinctively what feels right for you. I don't like the lean-back style of cruisers. I have short arms and dislike feeling so stretched. I also find it harder to steer with my arms fully extended.

I don't like leaning forward either. How does anyone ride a racer bike all day?! I sat on a Ducati once, just to see, and found it *so* uncomfortable. But that's me. You might climb on one and get tingles. You won't know till you try, so do it.

Test riding is the next step. It's great fun to do and again, you will instinctively know what feels right for you.

I didn't know anything about bikes when I bought mine, so I played safe and bought the same models I had been training on, a Honda CB125F then a Suzuki SFV650 (more usually called a Gladius) Some people will tell you 'Don't buy what you trained on. There will be another bike that is so much more 'You.' Maybe, but I still feel 100% that it was the right decision for me, both times.

Which brings me neatly to this...

Asking others for advice

It can be very useful, hearing the opinions of others, but ultimately it has to be *your* decision. Stick to your guns! Don't be pressured into buying a bigger bike than you feel comfortable with.

The pressure can come from partners or friends. 'Why are you looking at that? It's a child's bike' was the response I had from one friend when I told him I rather fancied a Honda Rebel 500.

I saw a woman come under pressure on a woman's page when she mentioned she was considering buying a 300cc for her first big bike.

Instantly the comments came:

'I think you might find 300 is not enough power....'

'You might quickly outgrow a 300cc...'

With respect to these women, this advice, though kindly meant, was nonsense. They were talking about how *they* felt about power. And it could mean the difference between someone buying a bike they love and doing thousands of miles, or buying a bigger bike that sits in the garage because they feel too scared to take it out.

The UK's testing system adds pressure too. You have to take your A licence on a 50kw minimum machine, which is usually a 650cc.

Consequently, anyone who has learned and passed on a 650 can feel reluctant to buy something smaller. I certainly felt that way, as if by buying say, a 500cc, I would be down-skilling.

Over in Spain, my friend Georgia trained and passed her A2 test on a 250cc bike. She bought a gorgeous-looking Suzuki Intruder 250 and, five years later, she still adores it. She has not outgrown it. She does not find it underpowered. She has travelled all around Spain on it and finds it nippy enough for central Barcelona too. It is perfectly suited to her needs.

The UK is so out of step with the rest of the world, manufacturers don't

HONDA REBEL 500

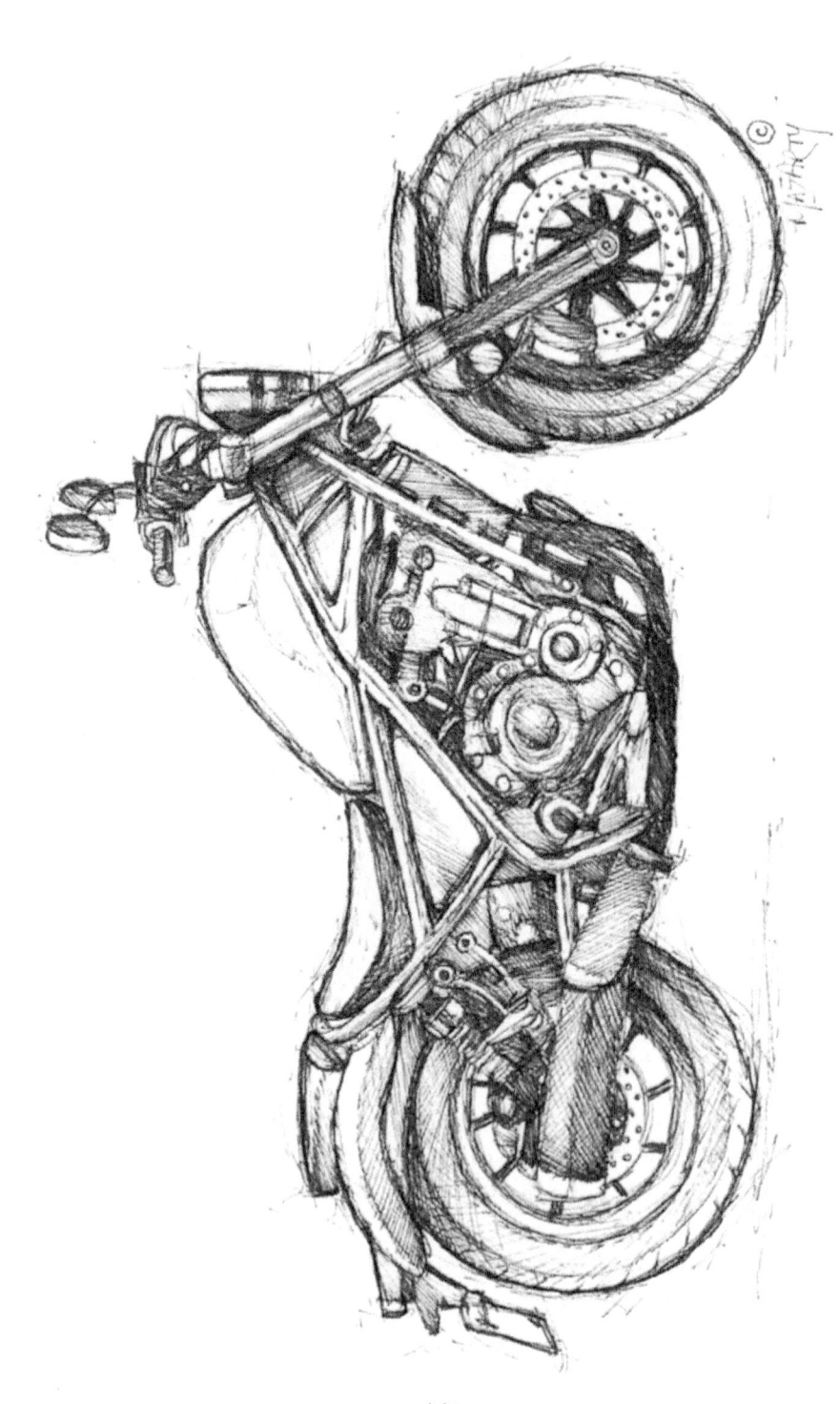

even offer Brits their full range of models. When I spoke to my local Honda dealer about the Rebel, I was amazed to learn there is a 350cc version which sells really well abroad.

'Why don't they sell them here?' I asked.

'No one would buy it,' he said. 'Not when they can have a 500 on their licence. That's the reasoning, anyway.'

This is such a shame, because I imagine it's a great bike. The Rebel 500 is enormous fun, and one of the easiest bikes I have ever ridden.

If you fancy a 350cc bike, go for it! I was in Thailand recently, and the Bangkok police were riding 300cc Hondas. There is *nothing* small about 200 - 500cc bikes.

Equally, don't let people talk you out of a *bigger* bike, if that is what you want and you truly feel you can handle it. Many women have bought an 800-1200cc bike as their first bike and never regretted it.

Getting it Wrong

One of my friends bought a Yamaha MT-07 for her first big bike. She was wildly excited about it and felt confident, having learned on one.

She sold it within six months. 'The torque was too much for me,' she said. 'It had to go.' Instead she had bought a Rebel 500 and was *loving* it.

When I was buying my Gladius, I saw an immaculate one listed by a woman rider. She had owned it for six months, her first big bike. It had every add-on available but astonishingly low mileage. She wrote in the listing: 'I am heartbroken to be selling but have finally admitted to myself she is too big for me.'

I can understand this. I learned on a Gladius, but there is a world of difference between riding one in the supportive company of your instructor and taking one out on your own.

Six months seems to be a checkpoint for first bikes. The honeymoon is over - how do you feel about it now? Are you joyfully clocking up the miles and building confidence? Or are you finding excuses not to go out?

We all make mistakes. Don't let this set you back. Remember your dream of freedom and make it happen. Sell the bike and get another.

'I am a short rider. Any suggestions....?'

It can be very helpful to ask other women for suggestions, especially if you are a shorter rider. Being able to put your feet down is reassuring. But remember that everyone is talking about *their* experience. How they felt when they were starting out or how they feel now. They are not you.

'I am 5' 1" and ride a (insert name here)' they will write. 'I can flat foot easily. Great bike!' Often there will be a photo of a glorious-looking cruiser. It looks perfect until you pull up the specs on Google and find it weighs 250kg. No problem for an experienced rider who knows how to manual handle heavy machines. But do you want to be manoeuvring that in an Aldi car park on your own on a wet Wednesday? Possibly not.

Comfort is something that varies wildly from person to person. It also depends on how long you ride for. I like to tour, so I need a bike that is comfortable for six hours a day, every day. I know that if I asked online, I would get recommendations from people who ride for a couple of hours on a Sunday. It's all well-meant, but you do have to read with a questioning mind.

'Great first bike' is something you see a lot in listings. Most commonly it will be a 650, the kind you learned on. SV650s, MT-07s ... They are powerful bikes. My Gladius goes from 70 mph up to 95 in a heartbeat. I love that but it might scare the pants off you.

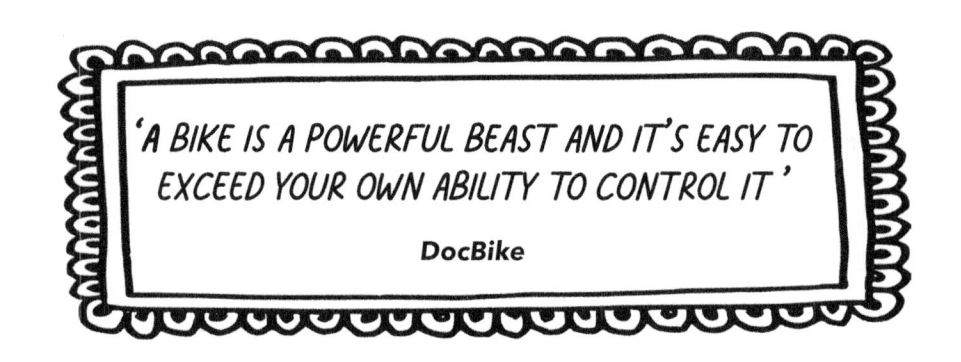

> **'A BIKE IS A POWERFUL BEAST AND IT'S EASY TO EXCEED YOUR OWN ABILITY TO CONTROL IT'**
>
> **DocBike**

Most people have far more power in their bikes than they need. Many have more than they can safely handle. The general advice for a beginner is look for a bike that is under 80 bhp (brake horsepower) That is considered 'manageable' power for someone new to riding. Forget the cc for a moment, that is misleading. The cc (cubic capacity) refers to the capacity of the engine, not the power. A 600cc bike can have much more power than a 900cc.

Over in Europe, they don't talk much about cc at all. They talk about how many kilowatts (kw) a bike has. That again is a power measurement.

To find a bike's information online, use the word 'specs' (specifications) eg 'Gladius 650 specs.' This will bring up the bhp, the torque, the cc and the weight. Torque is how hard the engine can push your forward. Dry weight is without petrol, wet weight is with a full tank.

If you want something that looks great but isn't too powerful, look at Royal Enfield bikes. A 650cc Interceptor is 47 bhp. A Triumph Speed

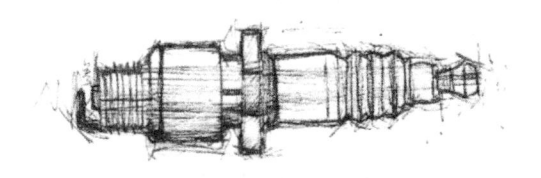

Twin 900 (formerly called the Street Twin) is a popular first choice for women. That is 54 bhp.

For comparison, a Suzuki Gladius is 71 bhp. A Yamaha MT-07 is 74 bhp.

'But I *want* a Fireblade....'

There's nothing to stop you having one. Some women are very confident riders from the start. They buy a bike that would *terrify* me, then ride off happily into the sunset. If that's your dream, go for it. I won't tell you to be careful, because you'll be sick of hearing that already, I guess!

> 'IT'S EASY TO OVER-PLAN AND TAKE THE ADVENTURE OUT OF THINGS. I USED TO THINK NO FURTHER THAN I COULD SEE'
>
> **Elspeth Beard, author of Lone Rider**

PART 15: LIFE AS A NEWLY QUALIFIED RIDER

Getting Beeped

No one likes being beeped by drivers. Whether it's a short toot or a long blast, it's upsetting and can send your confidence into freefall.

When I wrote the blog **Losing the L plates** (see earlier) I had just passed my Mod 2. Now, more than a year later, I can say that drivers definitely *did* cut me some slack as a visible learner. On a big bike, without plates, you are expected to be competent and confident on the road. If not, chances are you'll get a blast of the horn.

I find it upsetting when I feel it's unfair. When I'm trying to do something that was challenging for me: a very bendy road or a steep, winding descent. When it's wet and I've slowed down for safety's sake. Drivers have no understanding of how damned hard it can be on a bike.

Once I was on my 125 and was caught on a road that had such a gusting cross wind, I was genuinely scared the bike would go down from under me. I'm not an idiot - I was fully aware my speed had dropped to 20 mph; I could see the queue building behind me; I could see they were unable to overtake because it was single carriageway and busy; I knew it was a weekday and people were wanting to get to places. I was scanning the road ahead, desperately looking for somewhere I could pull in but it wasn't possible. I could only keep going.

Finally I saw a lay-by ahead. It was rough and gravelly, but I pulled into it nonetheless. And sure enough, as the first of the cars overtook me,

I received a long blast of horn, despite the L plates.

At moments like that, when I'm trying my best and wishing with all my heart it could just be over, it feels grossly unfair that some impatient so-and-so should be hassling me. *I have a right to be here, on this road*, I tell myself. *I want to get home in one piece today. If I need to go at this speed, I will.*

You've probably had moments like this too. Surely everyone does, especially in the beginning.

But there are other times when I've been beeped and felt it was entirely justified. Sometimes I *do* dawdle, pootling along below the national speed limit. That's fine when I'm out in the countryside with no one behind me, but not on a road with traffic. My trainer Laura constantly urged me to get up to the national limit and stay there, even when I didn't want to.

Think for a moment how it feels to be stuck behind a driver who is doing thirty five on a perfectly clear road. Yes, they might have their reasons but it's still annoying if you're trying to get somewhere and it forces you into overtaking.

This is why we are taught to ride to the nationals. Pootle along and you become, in effect, a hazard that others will have to deal with.

I have also had long blasts of the horn for endangering other drivers. I confess I have done moves that were verging on suicidal. The one in France, where I swooped across four lanes of motorway at 90mph to reach an exit instantly leaps to mind. Boy, did I deserve the ire of that lorry driver.

Without exception, all my dangerous moves were done because I was following someone else, trying to keep up. This is why riding with others increases your risk of an accident so significantly. You know the Golden Rule - ride your own ride - but believe me, it is *very* easy to forget it when you see your partner suddenly dive for a turning you weren't expecting. My crazy brain seems to put 'don't lose him' above everything else. Brains work so fast, it takes only a second for mine to compute *you will be on your own/ the next junction could be miles away/ he won't be able to turn around and find you/ you have no comms or satnav* and before I know it, I'm doing whatever it takes to make the turn too. Hard last minute braking, cutting in front of others, whatever. It is *so* dangerous.

Being beeped is something you have control over. If you are beeped on a ride, let it go - ride on. Reflect on it once you are safely home. Be honest. Put yourself in the driver's seat. Were you day-dreaming a bit? Was it an unsafe or unexpected manoeuvre? If so, try to do better next time.

Remember you don't know what was in the driver's head when they beeped. Sometimes people beep because you gave them a fright or because they want to tell you 'that really wasn't safe.' It isn't always a rebuke. It can be a pure emotional response.

According to the Highway Code, the horn is only to be used to warn others of your presence. If you ride abroad, you'll find they use their horns far better than we do. Often it means 'I'm coming through.' In India, for example, it is usual to use your horn before overtaking. Lorries frequently have SOUND YOUR HORN written on their tailgates to remind drivers to do it. In Thailand, drivers sometimes gave me three short beeps on their horn as they overtook, warning me they were there. I suspect they weren't convinced I'd seen them. They were usually right on this! Thai drivers will overtake you without leaving the lane if the traffic is busy so they pass *really* close. They also beep on hairpins to say 'I'm coming through on your side of the road.'

Curiously, in all the time I was riding in Thailand, I never heard a horn blared in anger. Ever. Even in rush hour Bangkok. I was also never hassled for going slow on bendy stretches of road. This is because every driver has spent time on a scooter. They understand how it feels to be on two wheels. How wonderful is that?

When Your Confidence Goes In Reverse

It's comforting to believe that once you have a full licence and get your first big bike, it will be easy and joyful.

It won't. There will be many days like that, but there will also be stinkers. Days when nothing seems to go right, or you have a heart-stopping moment, or the sheer effort reduces you to tears or …. The list is endless! And everyone *will* have these days, no matter how experienced they are. It is part of being a rider.

But these are individual days. I experienced something more and, having spoken to friends, it seems others have battled it too. It is when your confidence seems to go in reverse.

Here's how it was for me.

I passed my Mod 2 in September and did a few thousand miles before putting my bike into winter storage. I felt strong, confident and happy. But in the spring, when I returned to riding, something had changed.

The more I rode, the more hazardous the roads seemed to be. Even when I was driving my car, I couldn't help noticing dangerous road surfaces and hilly junctions, thinking how nightmarish it would be to encounter them on my bike. I started to avoid roads I had previously ridden on my 125.

It was like I had seen too much. The more experience I gained, the more anxious I became. By now, I had found a permanent garage for my bike. Just manoeuvring her out of there made me *so* anxious, I would feel my heart beating in my chest.

One day I had to go to Devon on business. I went in the car, but it was exactly the same route I had done on my bike just a few months earlier. I looked at the hilly junctions, the bends, the motorway roundabouts and couldn't *believe* I had ever ridden this route with ease and confidence. I felt I couldn't begin to attempt it now.

One of my friends told me she went through a very similar experience. She reached the point where she very nearly gave up. It's weird, but you start to question whether motorcycling is meant for you after all. You've spent all that money, done all that training, passed all those tests, but maybe…you were wrong.

If this is you at the moment, I urge you to KEEP GOING. You will get through it. **How to Push Through It** will help

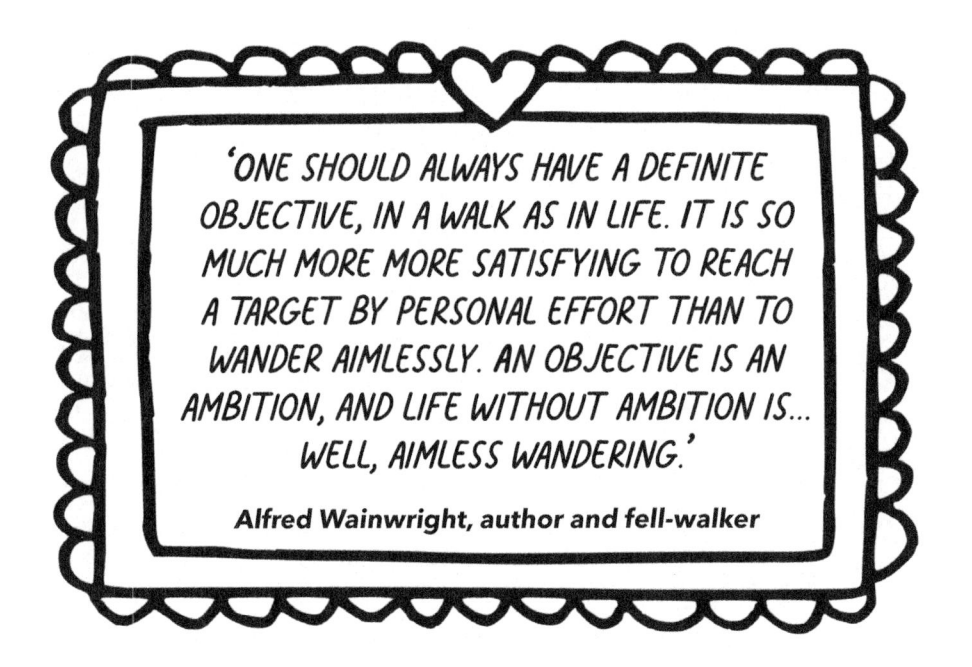

> 'ONE SHOULD ALWAYS HAVE A DEFINITE OBJECTIVE, IN A WALK AS IN LIFE. IT IS SO MUCH MORE MORE SATISFYING TO REACH A TARGET BY PERSONAL EFFORT THAN TO WANDER AIMLESSLY. AN OBJECTIVE IS AN AMBITION, AND LIFE WITHOUT AMBITION IS… WELL, AIMLESS WANDERING.'
>
> **Alfred Wainwright, author and fell-walker**

'Help! I don't know where to go…'

I once read an interesting post from a woman who wasn't riding because she had no idea where to go. This resonated with me because while I knew plenty of places I could go, I had been to them so often, the novelty had worn off.

If you go out regularly, you can soon become very familiar with the roads in your area, and there's only so far you can go in a day. If you're out with friends or a partner, you'll have fun wherever you go. But for a solo rider, it can be harder. I definitely went through a phase of aimless wandering and didn't enjoy it. I much prefer to ride with purpose.

If you have no idea where to go, do a bit of research and find destinations to head for. Places to visit, whether they are tea rooms, gardens, retail parks or whatever.

In my first year of riding, when I was on my 125, I was a member of the National Trust. This was brilliant for giving me somewhere to aim for. Within my ride-out radius, there are a dozen NT places, all with fabulous gardens and cafes. I love gardens, and since they change with the seasons, there was always something new to see. I'd take a stroll, enjoy a pot of tea or an ice cream then ride on. Sometimes I would plan a route that took in two or three properties. Not having to pay an entry fee every time made that possible.

If old houses or gardens aren't your thing, what do you like? Plan your journey around that. It's having a sense of purpose that is important, not the destination.

I am fond of Gregg's cheese and onion pasties, and there's a Gregg's seventeen miles away from my home. Very often I make that my destination! It's a lovely route across country, with plenty of bends to practise on. I can do the round trip in about an hour and a half, including the tea break. Though it often takes me much longer... Once I'm out, I ride on and on, taking whichever road takes my fancy.

Once you're riding like that, it doesn't feel aimless, even though it's wandering. It feels pleasurable.

Many riders head for biker cafes. Don't be put off by the idea. They're not all greasy spoons, packed with hordes of hairy bikers. Some are at interesting locations, like airfields. You can sit with a coffee and watch gliders taking off. How relaxing is that? You'll soon find ones you like.

As usual, women's groups online are a good source of information. Say you're stuck for places to go and suggestions will roll in. You might get women offering to ride with you too; you will not be the only one wanting to get out more often.

Going Widdershins

After a while, you might find you're doing the same few circular routes all the time. If they start to feel boring, try travelling in the opposite direction. It's like having a completely new road! All the bends feel unfamiliar and you see fresh things.

I spend a lot of time studying Google maps to find new routes. The other day, I decided to ride to my favourite cafe but told myself I had to find a totally new route to it. It turned out to be a fantastic road with glorious views. I felt like I was on my holidays!

Start a New Journal

Another way to stop aimless wandering is to return to focussed practice.

Whenever I start to feel a bit 'drifty,' I turn to my journal. It's a bit different to the one I kept as a learner. At the end of a ride-out I write a entry containing these things:

- A **general note** on where I went

- **Three things I really enjoyed about the day** (non-technical things eg the walnut cake in the cafe, the feeling of freedom)

- **Three things I did well** (technical things eg *Perfect hill start on*

Cleeve Hill)

- **Three things needing attention** (technical eg *'Bit of a fumbled stop when I reached the roundabout at the top of the exit ramp…)*
- **Action Plan** (three clear tasks)

Note that it's not three things I did *badly*. Keep it positive. Next time you're heading out, look at the action plan and make this the focus for your ride.

Make sure you date the entries. Be creative! I like to draw diagrams, use different coloured felt tips and always add star stickers.

Looking back on previous entries is fascinating. It's brilliant for showing you how far you've come and what enormous progress you're making.

Return to the Industrial Estate

Once you've passed your Mods, it is shockingly easy for your hard-won slow manoeuvring skills to fall away from you.

I remember how liberating it felt to do a 'fail' u-turn, a day or so after passing. The road ahead was completely closed because of roadworks; I had no option but to go back the way I'd come. Compared to the Mod 1 test area, I had a *huge* amount of room to make the turn - two full lanes. I could easily have done it as I'd learned. Instead, I did a bit of slow paddling, then a bit of a swing round with my foot pushing the ground, scooter-style, and I was off and away. It felt deliciously naughty.

Unfortunately, it soon became a habit. Within a month, I had completely lost the ability to do a tight u-turn and the confidence to even attempt it. A *month!*

So what? you might say. You can still turn around. It's not important how you do it. And how often do you need to do u-turns anyway?

The answer, for me at least, is nearly every time I go for a ride. I make wrong turns and have to double-back. I park in car parks where the easiest way to exit would be to do a u-turn. I find the road ahead is unexpectedly blocked. I take a detour to a favourite cafe with no car park, knowing I will need to return the same way I came.

The list goes on...

If you are on your own, you can go round the block or up to the next roundabout to avoid u-turning. But if you are with others, it just isn't an option.

For me, it came to a head when I was in Italy with my buddy Frank. He u-turns all the time. He thinks nothing of it, throwing his bike around like it's a toy. So whenever he took a wrong turn, he would pull over then u-turn and expect me to follow.

I would sit there looking at the road in a panic. Was there a turning up ahead? Could I maybe...? Usually I had to just do it. Every time my confidence failed me and I would resort to some kind of paddling. I would get round. But the truth was, it was stressy and dangerous. Cars don't expect to find a bike doing a shaky three-point turn in the middle of the road. I was making myself so vulnerable, and paddling is not a stable thing to do at the best of times.

It left me feeling like a complete idiot. I was angry at myself for letting the skills slip away. I had paid so much money and spent so much time practising - for what? To be this incompetent and fearful? Because it *was* fear - again. Fear of dropping the bike, of getting it wrong, of not making it round.

I didn't want to be a fearful little mouse. I wanted to be like Steve McQueen in *The Great Escape*. I wanted to be able to get on my bike, turn and go. No problem, no stress.

So when I was home from the trip, I returned to the industrial estate where I had spent so many hours on my 125. I made myself do the circuits again. The figures of eight, the u-turns within the parking spaces. I forced myself to do tight turns.

Just the other day, I was out with my IAM observer, doing advanced training. He wasn't at all happy with the way I was turning right at junctions.

'You are *not* safe,' he said. 'You *cannot* do it like that. You need to go to a car park and practise, practise, practise. Do you have anywhere near you?'

I smiled. 'I know an industrial estate…..'

Confidence Hack: Run your own GPS

When you're tackling a very curvy road, especially one with nasty hairpins, it's easy to become over-cautious. I used to find myself slowing down at every bend, just in case it turned out to be a tricky one.

The way to stop this is to run your own GPS, even if you are following someone who is navigating. It will show you what is coming, giving you plenty of time to prepare.

Perhaps even more importantly, it shows you what *isn't* coming! Instead of the horrors you're imagining, it lets you know you can relax for a bit - the road ahead is straighter for a while.

The first time I did this, I found it totally liberating. The ride became infinitely less stressy and far more enjoyable.

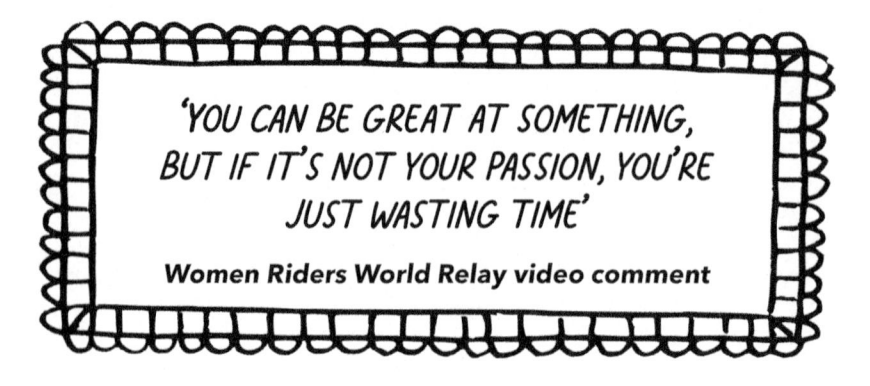

> 'YOU CAN BE GREAT AT SOMETHING, BUT IF IT'S NOT YOUR PASSION, YOU'RE JUST WASTING TIME'
>
> **Women Riders World Relay video comment**

PART 16: STOPPING RIDING

Women stop riding for many reasons, but usually it comes down to that thing called Life. Health, finances, family, work, relationships… When something changes, riding a bike might no longer be possible or even desirable. Many a bike has been sold to finance a holiday, a wedding or a new (equally expensive!) hobby.

But what if it's more personal than that? What if you can't stop thinking: *Is this for me?*

Many of us have been there. I've been there twice so far: the first time when I was struggling to learn the 125, the second time when I had my full licence but my confidence seemed to be draining out of me.

The good news is, you can get through it. I did, and I have talked to other women who pushed through it too.

How to push through

- You must **want to get through it.** I think this is really important. If you know in your heart you'd rather not be riding, you're going to be fighting an uphill battle.

- **Read your journal** If you feel like your progress is stalling, this will show you how far you've come. Progress is always slower once you have passed through the initial learning phase, whatever you are learning.

- **Write an enjoyment list** (see below) Remind yourself of why you started this journey and what pleasures it has brought you so far.

- **Consider changing your bike,** especially if it is your first bike.

It's time to be brutally honest. Is it the right bike for you? How do you feel when you climb onto the saddle? Do you feel confident in your ability to handle it? Forget your dreams - is it too tall / powerful / heavy for you?

There is no shame in getting a smaller bike. Many, many women say they changed their bike and it transformed their riding experience. The bike most commonly mentioned is the Honda Rebel 500. It is very low, very light and very easy to ride. Royal Enfields are easy to ride too. Check out the Meteor 350.

- **Do a road trip.** You need to feel bonded with your bike, like the bike is an extension of you. You're a team. The best way of bonding is to travel. It's about staying in the saddle and clocking up those miles together.

A road trip also brings an enormous sense of achievement. You'll be out of your comfort zone but you will cope. Sometimes you achieve more than you ever dreamed possible.

Setting yourself a fresh challenge might be all you need to push through. It doesn't need to be a really long trip. An overnight break can be enough. You simply need to go further than you would normally go in a day.

- **Join a women's group**. Female biker friends can make a huge difference. It's not just about the riding, it's about the talking. Over coffee and cake, you'll find you are not alone in experiencing anxiety and doubt. You'll get friendly help, advice, reassurance and lots of laughter too. I am a member of Curvy Riders. There are meet-ups all year round; in the winter, we drive to places for lunch if the weather is too bad for riding.

- **Try therapy**. This can be especially useful if an accident or near-miss has affected your confidence. I found WingWave worked wonders for me (see **WingWave**) NLP (Neuro Linguistic Programming) can work too.

The End of the Road

Like any pastime, riding is supposed to bring you pleasure. It should be fun. It should make you happy. If it doesn't, maybe it is time to let it go.

There is no shame in stopping riding. Let's get positive, right now.

YOU HAVEN'T GIVEN UP. You are no longer riding. No more, no less.

'Giving up' suggests you've failed - when you haven't. You have achieved so much more than you are giving yourself credit for.

- You turned a dream into a reality. You did something that thousands of people, men and women, only dream about.

- You rode a motorcycle. If you did a CBT and rode a 125, you have ridden a motorcycle. On your own. Think about that.

- You have courage. Simply climbing onto the bike took courage. Riding on a public road for the first time can be scary as hell. But if you did a CBT, you did that. You dug deep and found your courage.

- You're not weak. You've been on an incredible journey, exploring the world of motorcycling. Now you have made the decision to move on. Making that decision is a positive move, a show of strength.

- You are not letting anyone down. You did your best. No one can do any more than that. I appreciate that it can be really hard when a partner is involved. Sometimes partners have it all mapped out: what trips you will make together, what bike you will ride, how fast you will learn. They assume you will enjoy it as much as they do. Bringing an end to all that can be tough. But you cannot live your life for someone else's pleasure. You cannot *risk your life* for someone else's pleasure. If someone genuinely cares for you, they will support your decision. They will want you to be happy.

- You are choosing to move forward. Why leave a bike sitting in a garage unused? Selling it will release money to explore something else or fix a problem. You are taking control of your life.

Negative →	Positive
I've given up riding	I am no longer riding
I failed	I rode
I tried	I explored

You do not need to explain to people why you are stopping. It is your business, not theirs.

You do not need to apologise to anyone. People's feelings are *their* responsibility, not yours. If they are disappointed, sad or angry, that is for them to deal with, not you.

Make an Enjoyment List

Make a list of all the positive things that came out of the experience. Be specific. Remember the details. Smile!

What did you enjoy?
The ride to Scarborough with Jo and Sal. The feeling of freedom. The excitement of getting my 125

What did you achieve?
I rode to Mum's house on my own in the rain.

What did you learn about yourself?
I thought I would go to pieces if I fell off, but when it actually happened, I just picked the bike up and got back on.

CELEBRATE YOUR JOURNEY, CELEBRATE YOU

PART 17: KEEPING SAFE

Danger - The Facts

It's tempting to believe that women don't die on bikes. They don't suffer life-changing injuries. That happens only to men.

Sadly, it's not true.

It's also tempting to believe that crashes mostly happen at high speed. That if we take it steady, we'll be fine.

In fact, the majority of accidents happen under 35 mph. The most dangerous place for a rider to be is at a junction in a built-up area.

When you do the Bike Safe course, the police send you the breakdown figures. They make fascinating reading. Urban riding is #1 in the league. At #2 is country lanes. An extraordinarily high percentage of accidents involve only the motorcyclist. Many of these are country lane accidents. Trees and walls are very unforgiving.

Motorways are surprisingly safe, presumably because bikers are often in the fast lane rather than dodging between slow lorries. Less surprising is the fact that a motorway collision is more likely to be fatal or life-changing than an urban one.

The most likely time to die is between 3 - 5 pm on a Sunday: weekend riders, getting tired after a long day in the saddle, heading for home. Top of the range bike, expensive gear... It didn't save them.

We all know it's dangerous. So is life. My ex brother-in-law died after falling off a ladder in his back garden. All we can do is ride responsibly, be aware of the facts and **keep training.** Training gives you new skills and keeps you sharp. Biking is a lifelong practice, like yoga. You wouldn't do six lessons of yoga then say 'All done!' would you?

If you aren't well-trained, you are trusting to luck to keep you safe. Don't rely on something that can run out.

Listen To Your Body

It's a Hollywood thing, isn't it? Some guy has an argument (because it's always a guy) then roars off into the night on his bike, fired up with anger, despair, loss, a desire for revenge, whatever. He never has an accident. He rides like a god, faultlessly.

In the real world, the advice is very different. Never ride if you are feeling upset, sick, drunk, drugged or unbalanced. Bikes are very different to cars. They are far less forgiving of mistakes.

Don't Ride Beyond Your Ability

'It's okay - I've watched a YouTube video'

A friend told me her husband and his mates had recently returned from a trip to the Pyrenees in Spain, where they had ridden the high mountain passes. Afterwards, the general feeling was it had been 'too much.'

These were experienced riders, riding for decades. They had been on European road trips before. But still…

It's true, we have to move out of our comfort zone to learn. We need to tackle new challenges to progress. But one step at a time is the way to do it, whatever our level.

The ski-ing world has a great system. Recognising it is dangerous, they have a colour code system in place. In Europe, if you are a complete beginner, you stick to green slopes until you have the skill level required for blue (still classed as beginner) Then you progress to red (intermediate) black/ black single diamond (expert) and finally black double/triple diamond (extreme)

Motorbiking has no such system. You can pass your Mod 2 on Monday and head for the Alps on Tuesday. *Vrooom!* From green to black diamond overnight. No wonder accidents happen.

When I took my first tumble, I was riding beyond my skill level:

- → I was on an unfamiliar bike that I was struggling to control even on the flat.
- → I was on a tight, twisting mountain road.
- → There was frost. I had never ridden in the winter.
- → It was Italy. I was having to negotiate every corner on the other side of the road.
- → I had had my full licence for barely three months.

I was a Blue rider on a Red run.

I find it deeply unpleasant when I have to ride beyond my ability. I get no pleasure in being on a mountainous road with steep drops and no safety barrier.

People have said to me: 'Oh, but the feeling of elation when you've done it will be brilliant!! You'll feel so proud!'

Maybe I will feel like that in time. But right now, when I do roads like that, I am just glad to get to the end of them.

I am working on it. I push myself to do more challenging routes, because I want to enjoy it more. I want to experience that feeling of flow that everyone talks about, when you're able to swoop around bends with certainty and ease.

You don't have to go to the Alps to find challenging roads. When you're a beginner, a local hill can feel like a Black run! If I am riding with a buddy, I make sure he understands this. I don't want to be led down roads that will scare the bejeezus out of me. That is not how I learn.

Protect Your Phone

If you have an accident, you might need to call for help, so keep your phone safe. They are easily shattered in a tumble if they are attached to the handlebars. If you need GPS, it is better to buy a SatNav than use your phone.

Be careful where you store sharp items. I chatted to a man who had been forced off his bike by a lorry at 60mph. As he picked himself up off the road, he felt wetness and discovered his house keys (which had been in his jeans pocket) had embedded themselves into his stomach. This was his only injury.

If you are always carrying things, look at getting a top box or panniers. If you wear a backpack, imagine you took a tumble and fell backwards onto it. What are you carrying in there?

Ongoing Training

'Just because you've ridden for thirty years doesn't make you an advanced rider. An advanced rider is one who has done advanced training'

Simon Hayes, Motorcycle Riders Hub

I love advanced training sessions. I would do one every week if I could afford it.

Why? I love the focus it brings to my riding. I love working on my skill level - we can always be better riders. I want to be safe on the road, and that is what advanced training teaches.

When should I start advanced training?

You can start as soon as you have your full licence. If your journey to a full licence has been swift, think about it sooner rather than later. DAS training is fairly basic. It is designed to get you to test standard. There is *so much more* you can learn. I had great DAS training but I didn't learn about the importance of the rev counter until I stepped up to advanced. That transformed how I rode overnight. I didn't learn how to overtake until I did my advanced lessons. (Hands up if you just hit the throttle and go for it?)

It is never to late to start advanced training. I have been in classes with people who have ridden for decades without any formal training. Just yesterday, I was in a group with a lovely man who wrote in his evaluation: *'I have learned more in my two days training than I have in 20+ years of riding'*

It is also great fun! It is thrilling to ride in a group in tight, disciplined formation, with everyone knowing exactly where they should be positioned. You meet new people, make new friends, find riding buddies, all while you're improving.

How good do I need to be?

You need to be able to handle your bike confidently. You will be expected to ride to the national speed limit and you will be overtaking on single-lane roads, not just dual carriageways. They will train you in this but you must feel ready and willing to learn.

You need to have got past the stage where you are talking yourself through every junction. Once you are beyond that stage (and it will come, I promise!) riding becomes joyous and you will thrive on new challenges.

Advanced training doesn't feel the same as doing your DAS. It feels like a ride-out, not a lesson. It will push you but it should feel exciting, not stressy. Learning through fear is not the best method, despite what they say on those SAS tv programmes!

How can I do advanced training?

Good training schools will offer training up to advanced level. There are also various national groups that will have a branch local to you. IAM (Institute of Advanced Motorists) and RoSPA (Royal Society for the Prevention of Accidents) are the best-known. You will pay a one-off fee that includes the cost of your test, which you prepare for by going out on observed rides with one of their voluntary trainers. Although they are volunteers, they have all been through the system ahead of you. Some are ex-police. Their aim is to raise your standard of riding in various categories, like road positioning, observation and use of gears. When they feel you are test-ready, you will do an on-road test, just like a Mod 2.

The groups are very social too, organising ride-outs at the weekend and social meets in the evenings. Once you have passed your test, you need only pay a much smaller annual fee to remain part of the group.

It is also worth noting that many bike insurers offer a discount if you have passed with IAM or RoSPA. Remember to tell them!

Bike Safe and Biker Down

Bike Safe and Biker Down are training courses offered by the police and the fire service.

Bike Safe isn't free, but that doesn't stop it being *very* popular. Waiting lists are common. It is run by volunteer police riders and (sometimes) IAM observers.

The day begins with a classroom session covering hazards, cornering, road positioning etc. Then you join a police rider to go out for an observed ride. You will get a written assessment and a chat about your riding too.

It's fun - I recommend it. Many riders do it every few years as a refresher.

I enjoyed **Biker Down** even more, though that was probably because it was held in a fire station and we had a chance to see the fire engine (though sadly not the firemen!) up close.

Biker Down is entirely classroom-based. Through slides and chat, it looks at what to do if you are first on the scene at an accident involving a motorcyclist. It's not gory in any way. It covers CPR but not how to deal with wounds - they advise taking a first aid course to learn that. It's more to do with keeping the rider safe and what you need to tell the emergency services.

Again, I really enjoyed it and would recommend it. It is free to attend.

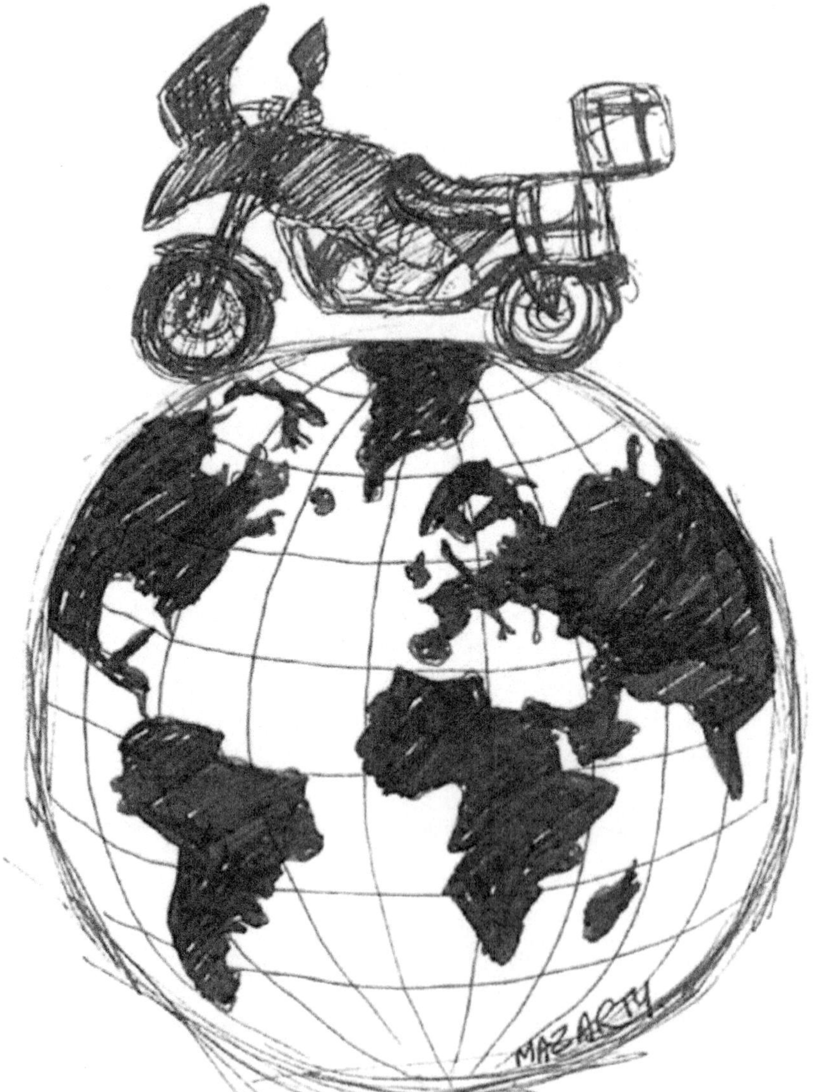
MAZARTY

PART 18: ROAD TRIPPING ABROAD

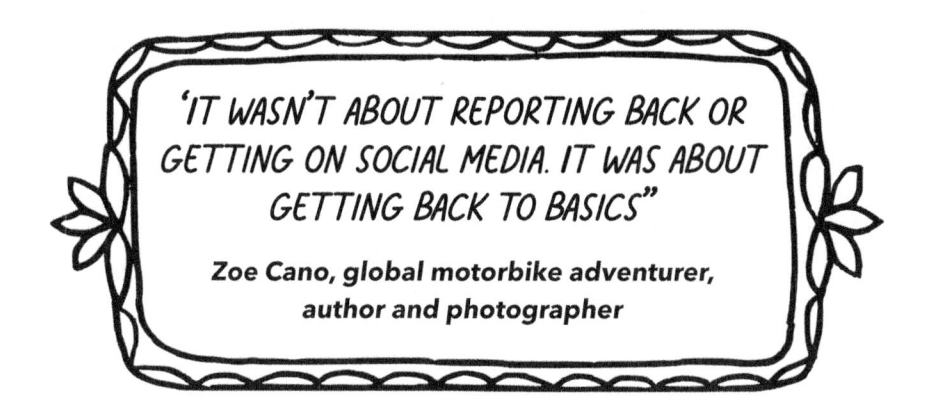

> *'IT WASN'T ABOUT REPORTING BACK OR GETTING ON SOCIAL MEDIA. IT WAS ABOUT GETTING BACK TO BASICS"*
>
> **Zoe Cano, global motorbike adventurer, author and photographer**

I am frankly amazed that this chapter exists. I can't believe I have a European road trip under my belt, when I've had my full licence barely a year. I've said it before in this book, but I'll say it again: hold onto your dreams and make them happen. You can achieve things much sooner than you imagined, and with more ease than you thought possible.

Many people have asked me for tips for first-time travellers, so here are some things I learned along the way that might be useful.

For a fuller account of my trip, see **My First European Trip**

Things I Learned

1. **You don't need an adventure bike**

My Suzuki Gladius 650 was the smallest bike on the Eurotunnel train, both ways. Most of the guys had huge tourers with lockable metal boxes. I had a couple of throw-over Oxford panniers and an Indian cotton bag held on with bungees.

On the Italian ferries, there was a dazzling array of adventure bikes:

KTMs, Africa Twins, Teneres... Huge things, like metal antelopes.

I had no envy for any of these bikes. My Suzuki did the job brilliantly. She handled the fast motorways with ease (those she was flung about by the wind somewhat) She was incredibly comfortable. I did six hours in the saddle some days and never had a sore backside. She carried my luggage perfectly. She was economical. Best of all, she was nippy and manoeuvrable in the cities.

She definitely handled the bends better than I did!

I saw no female riders on the crossings except a Spanish woman on a Harley, looking super-cool with her hair tied back in black bandana. I asked her if she had any trouble on the twisties with the Harley.

'She's not keen,' she laughed. 'But I haven't come off yet!'

If you dream of going abroad, don't tell yourself you'll go when you get a 'proper' touring bike. You don't need one.

2. **Eurotunnel and Ferry Crossings**

Like so many things, these are not as bad as you imagine. I imagined all kinds of nightmarish challenges, from slippery slopes to bolts on the floor that would shred my tyres. You *do* have to take care. But the good news is, boarding and disembarking are a fast process. You've done it before you realise. You can do this!

- **Keep your visor up**. You need to be as alert as possible.

- **Hold your ground**. This one is key if you are at all nervous. Ferry workers will try to hurry you along. There will lots of waving you forward and pointing. Ignore that. Do not ascend or descend a ramp until you are ready. I had a rule: I would not begin until the ramp ahead of me was clear. I did *not* want to be forced to stop midway - there was every chance I would drop the bike under those circumstances. I kept to this rule and it worked.

On a Sardinian ferry, exiting was chaos, with bikes and cars everywhere. I stopped at the top of the internal ramp and waited to descend. And bless him, a German biker pulled alongside, nodded and waited with me, holding back the other bikers till I'd started my descent. I hadn't spoken to him previously, he simply helped. You will be helped too.

I was lucky: the weather was dry and so were the ramps. Be VERY careful in the wet. There is grip on the ramps but seasoned travellers all say the same thing - they can get *very* slippery with water and spilled diesel. Riders do drop bikes on ferries, especially if they are heavy with luggage.

- **Keep up with the other riders when exiting abroad.** When I took the Eurotunnel to Calais, I was the last one to board the train. When the train arrived in France, I discovered I had to ride the entire length of the train, on the inside. There were bolts and ramps to avoid, so I took my time and emerged safely. But it meant that the other riders had all sped off and I had no idea where I was supposed to go. Also I had to ride on the other side of the road, and it is always easier to do that if you can follow others. So try to keep with the group, even if they are strangers.

- **You must be able to manual handle your bike.** Room is very tight and you must park where you are told. Don't worry about tying the bike down. Sometimes the workers do that for you. If not, other bikers will readily help if you ask them. There is enormous camaraderie on ferries and Eurotunnel.

Be aware that you might be expected to u-turn the bike to disembark. It depends on the ship's layout, but you will be going out the same way you came in.

- **You must be willing to do ramps.** This sounds obvious, but if you post your anxiety about ferries online, you will invariably get women who say they didn't have to do a ramp / they parked on the ground level / it was really easy because the bikes were boarded separately from the cars. That was true for them but it might not be true for you. Be realistic.

On the Sardinian ferry, the bikes were parked on Level 10. I had to ride up *two* internal ramps. And the bikes were boarded alongside cars, lorries, motorhomes, the lot. I handled it - as you will handle it. But be prepared for a full-on five minutes!

If you are with your partner and usually rely on them to do the tricky bits (you know who you are!) you will have to handle your own bike on ferries. It won't be possible for your partner to ride their bike up the ramp, park then come back down to ride yours up for you.

3. **European roads are fast**

Motorways abroad have very long access lanes, for good reason. The traffic is going *fast*. I regularly rode at 90 mph with overtakes at 100 mph. My riding buddy Frank, who is German, repeatedly told me off for joining (a) too soon and (b) too slowly. He told me to accelerate hard, get up to 70 mph and use the full length of the lane. That what it is there for, he said, and that is when drivers will *expect* you to join.

They will also expect you to use the middle and outside lanes for overtaking only. That middle lane cruising so beloved of UK drivers is *not* acceptable. You will soon be flashed.

Which leads me nicely onto….

4. **Italian bikers can scare the Bejeezus out of you**

Italian bikers routinely overtake other bikes in the outside lane if they want to go faster.

I was totally shocked the first time this happened. I was overtaking a lorry at the time, on a stretch of urban motorway. I had moved into the outside lane and was doing around 80 mph. Suddenly there was a flash of something to my left and a bike came between me and the central barrier. It roared past me at God knows what speed, leaving me truly shaken. I thought it was a one-off, some crazy guy racer. But no, it is what they do, especially in urban areas.

Scooters do it all the time in cities, overtaking you on both sides as you approach junctions. They will also steal any space, making it very hard to ride in the usual 'pair' position. Single lane makes no difference.

5. **The automated toll booths are incredibly fiddly to deal with**

Especially when you're wearing gloves. The toll motorways work like a car park: you take your ticket at a booth as you enter then re-insert it and pay as you leave. Many riders have a tank bag to hold the ticket and their credit card. I would have liked something attached to the inside of my screen. I was always fumbling with the zip of my jacket's side pocket while the cars lined up behind me.

6. **Petrol stations might not accept your pre-loaded travel card**

Many of the petrol stations are unmanned. You have to insert and authorise your card in a machine (or the pump itself) before filling up.

I soon discovered that my Post Office pre-loaded MasterCard would not authorise. It was fine at the toll booths on the motorway, great for purchases, but every petrol station machine refused it.

7. **To ride in European cities, you need to be able to handle your bike like it's a scooter**

Maybe it's different on a biking trip. Maybe you head for the countryside and stay in out-of-town hotels with easy access and parking. Maybe you don't ride with a German who thinks nothing of detouring into the middle of a city for a coffee break.

'Why not?' Frank would say.

Why not indeed. I confess it is delightful to find yourself unexpectedly having coffee and a croissant next to the leaning tower of Pisa. But it does mean you have to handle the challenges that come with it.

We visited a string of old cities - Rouen, Orleans, Bordeaux, Lyon, Foix, Troyes, Alghero, Carcassone, Chambery, Asti, and usually stayed in the Old Town. This meant cobbled streets, steep alleyways, constant stopping and starting, hordes of pedestrians and always being surrounded by a host of scooters. We frequently rode and parked on pavements.

Are you confident with u-turns? In Rouen centre, I twice had to do full u-turns at traffic lights. This wasn't because we'd taken a wrong turn, it was how the traffic flowed.

I used to ride pillion with a guy who would do everything in his power to avoid stopping at junctions on his top-heavy Suzuki V-Strom. I can't begin to imagine how he would cope with central Barcelona in July!

8. **Ashford Travelodge is a great place to stay if you're using Eurotunnel**

It's right next to Junction 9 on the M20, with Eurotunnel just a ten minute ride away at Junction 11a. If you need petrol, there's a Tesco superstore at Junction 10. Good parking, comfortable - and cheap!

9. **Regulations differ**.

Go online to check what you are supposed to carry with you. I took a hi-vis jacket and spare light bulbs to satisfy French officials, but not the breathalyser kit I was also supposed to have. You always need to carry your ownership document (original, not a photocopy) plus your insurance documents and driving licence. Your bike needs a UK sticker.

France is notoriously keen on rules. As we crossed the border from Italy into France, Frank was instantly pulled over by the police for not wearing gloves. Once he had produced them (from the very bottom of his saddlebag) he was allowed to ride on. They had no problem with the fact that he was riding a 1200cc scrambler in shorts, tee shirt and plimsolls. But no gloves? *Non, monsieur!*

Which brings me to….

10. **Gear or no gear?**

On a summer's day in Europe, you will always be able to spot the British riders. They will be the ones fully geared up from top to toe. Everyone else will be riding in shorts and tee shirts. Unless you are by the coast, where the girls will be in shorts and bikini tops.

I suspect this is partly because many riders begin with scooters, nipping around town with only a helmet added to their outfit. They move on to a bigger bike but the preference remains.

The only time you see otherwise is when you are heading for the hills and the biking routes, then you will see guys in their leathers. And they *are* overwhelmingly guys. In my month-long trip, I saw only three women riders on motorbikes though plenty on scooters in town.

I won't lie: I found wearing the gear the worst thing about my trip.

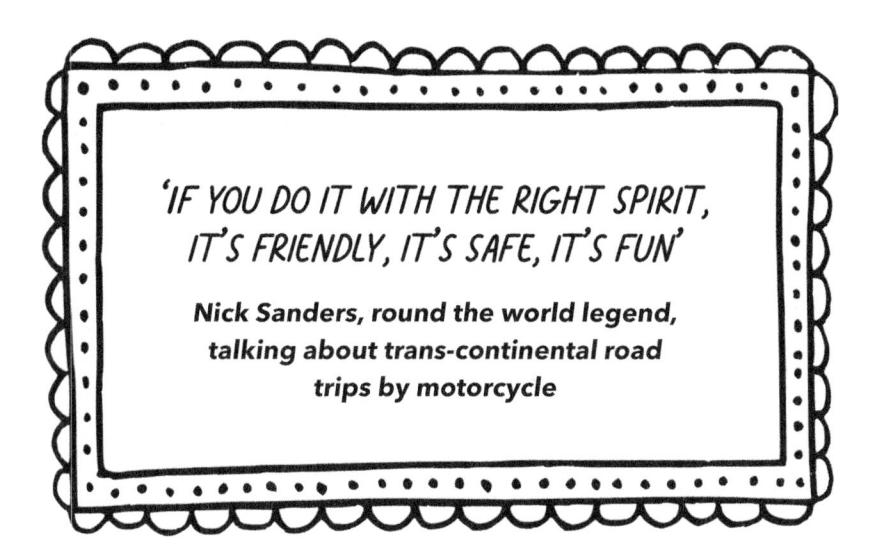

> '**IF YOU DO IT WITH THE RIGHT SPIRIT, IT'S FRIENDLY, IT'S SAFE, IT'S FUN**'
>
> **Nick Sanders, round the world legend, talking about trans-continental road trips by motorcycle**

Do I recommend a European road trip?

YES! It will be hard at times. You will be challenged daily. But the rewards are enormous. You will love it and come home hungry for more.

If you dream it, do it. You will handle it. Get out there and LIVE.

Here's a blog I wrote after I returned from my trip.

The Benefits of a European Road Trip

(August 2022)

Apart from the extraordinary sense of achievement, the wonderful things you'll see and do, the delicious food you'll eat, the astonishing roads you'll ride, the laughter and the memories that will last forever - is there any reason to go? Will it help improve your riding?

Yesterday I took my bike out for the first time since returning and was amazed at the difference in my riding. My cornering is vastly improved for starters. How could it not be, after all those Sardinian bends? But mostly I see the change in simply getting on and going. Not making a fuss. I seem far more at home on the bike.

It's the sheer repetition of actions that makes the difference. That's what builds muscle memory.

Over those thirty days, how many roundabouts did I do? How many hill starts? How often did I stop and start? How often did I park? How many times did I overtake? How many miles did

I filter? How many hills did I climb? How many mountains did I descend? How many bends did I turn?

How many new challenges did I experience and overcome? Cobbled streets and underground car parks. Riding the length of a train - on the inside! Riding at night for the first time. Staying with another rider through miles of dense urban traffic. All these things are embedded in my memory.

I feel I have no excuses now. Before the trip, I would avoid visiting friends because the entrance to their road was 'a bit tricky'. I avoided Burford for a year because it had a single sharp bend on the way in. <u>One sharp bend</u> That is unbelievable.

How can I ever question going up Malvern Hill when I've done a mountain pass in the Alps? How can I balk at Hereford when I've handled Lyon?

My world has exploded!

PART 19: WOMAN IN WHITE

A few years ago, I was stuck at a roundabout. It was one of those days when life was sitting heavy on my shoulders. I was alone, two hours from home and longing for a cup of tea.

It was a huge motorway roundabout with queues coming in from six different directions. Hundreds of cars were inching forward, going nowhere fast. I wound down the window to get a breath of air.

Then I heard a rumble behind me and a white racing bike cruised past my window. The rider was a woman, dressed completely in white: boots, leathers, helmet. As she passed, I saw a long blonde plait hanging down her back. It had a blue ribbon on the end.

When she reached the roundabout, she didn't stop. She curled around it like a cat and was off, onto the motorway beyond.

And I said to myself 'I want to be her.'

This summer, with my friend Frank, I found the courage to make my first European road trip. I rode through miles and miles of sunflower fields in France. I slept in a chateau, a sixteenth century loft and a Romany caravan in the middle of a vineyard. I rode through the Pyrenees to Barcelona and caught the ferry to Sardinia. There I rode along coastal roads, dancing between land and sea and sky. Back across to mainland Italy, I rode through the Italian Alps and thought my heart would explode with amazement at where I was and what I was doing - riding my own bike.

Midway along that pass through the Alps, we came to a lake so impossibly turquoise, it looked photo-shopped. I asked Frank to take my photo. I really wanted to capture the moment: this was one of the best days of my life.

Frank took the photo. That evening I saw it for the first time.

A woman in white, riding her own bike. Bold, strong, wild and free.

If I can do it, you can do it too.

SO DO IT!

RESOURCES

Curvy Riders

Look online if you want to make new friends to ride out with. There are groups nationwide. One will be perfect for you.

I am a member of Curvy Riders MCC. The Curvies are great because they are organised into regional groups - you will be able to meet up with women local to you. For a small annual fee, you can access all the regional Facebook pages. One fee covers as many regions as you want to join.

It's about socialising as well as riding. Meets continue throughout the winter - a weekend lunch gathering for example. It is perfectly fine to drive to a meet-up if the weather is bad. You don't *have* to ride.

You can join while still on a 125 though you'll need to check with the organiser before joining a ride-out. Sometimes motorways are involved.

Find them here: curvyriders.co.uk

Books

My instructor Laura Smith at WMT (Women's Motorcycle Training) has written a great booklet for anyone wanting to learn to ride. It explains the CBT, the Mods, what to look for in a training school and more. Very useful! Find it on Amazon: **Learn to Ride a Motorcycle for Women** by Laura Smith https://amzn.eu/d/04ubP6K

Training

Motorcycle Riding Hub offers superb online training. Their videos take you through all the tests, step by step. Its founder, Simon Hayes, was one of my instructors. He's a fabulous trainer. motorcycleridershub.co.uk

Gear

The Visorcat visor wipe system I mentioned can be found here: visorcat.com

For hair, look at the HighTail hair protector: hightailhair.com

Other options are Bunneze: bunneze.com or scrub caps, like medics wear: https://amzn.eu/d/aCoAo1x Thin neck tubes are available at buff.com

For clothing, many women love MotoGirl: motogirl.co.uk

Ladybiker, another female-run company, is also very well-respected: ladybiker.co.uk

Tests

All the information you need on the various licences (A1, A2, A) is here: gov.uk/ride-motorcycle-moped

For CBT information: gov.uk/motorcycle-cbt

The theory test app I used was Motorcycle Theory Test UK from Deep River Development. The logo was a white motorcycle inside a green square. It's well worth paying a few extra pounds to have the videos.

Therapy

I had WingWave from Deborah Clarke at Life Therapy Coaching: https://www.lifetherapycoaching.co.uk/coaching-wingwave/.

Deborah is based near Oxford. For a national list of coaches look at https://wingwave.com/en/.

WingWave is a type of Neuro Linguistic Programming. You will find many NLP practitioners online.

Online Women's Groups

There are countless groups on Facebook. Like any online group, you'll soon know if you've found your tribe or not. If you are a beginner, it's great to try some of these communities. They can be very supportive and helpful, though be aware that some of the technical advice you will be offered might not be appropriate for your level of riding. It is always kindly meant, but people soon forget how difficult it can be for beginners with rudimentary skills.

I wholly recommend Female Riders UK. Led by three wonderful admins, Denise, Anna and Andreea, it's a warm, highly supportive and inspiring group. Many of the riders have ridden for a long time or travelled widely, so it's a great place to ask for advice, from technical questions to track days and everything in between. Beginners are welcome too.

Another really good group is Female Bikers UK. Members of this group seem to be mostly learners, so if you're starting out and feeling alone, this could be perfect for you. It's very supportive and encouraging, with women talking about their tests, sharing anxieties, asking very basic questions etc.

On both these pages, you can ask if there is anyone local who would like to ride out with you. There will almost certainly be someone who is keen and at your level.

Festivals

I have always enjoyed the Women in Motorcycling Exhibition. It's a growing festival with a great team behind it. Currently it's a one-day event but if you camp, there is entertainment for two evenings too. Male partners are welcome. womenmoto.co.uk

Social Media

If you like following people on social media, check out Vanessa Ruck, also known as The Girl On A Bike. She is truly inspiring. I first heard her talk at the Adventure Bike Rider Festival (abrfestival.com) and was captivated by her story. thegirlonabike.com

Ruby Rides is very popular, especially with younger women who love racing bikes. rubyrides.co.uk

I don't watch many training videos online because I generally don't trust them. The only person I like is MotoJitsu, who is very no-nonsense and a strict disciplinarian. Practise, practise, practise is his mantra. He doesn't accept any excuses for poor riding. You need to work harder, that's all! His slow riding is especially inspiring. He can do the tightest of manoeuvres on bikes the size of space stations and make it look easy. motojitsu.com

MILESTONES

I've put these pieces at the end of the book because not everyone will want to read them. They are a mixed bag: thoughts, detailed test accounts, practical advice, blogs and journal extracts written for myself about first-time experiences.

But I know some people love to go deeper. They love to hear exactly how it was, because it helps them imagine how it might be for them, in the future. That can be reassuring.

So here are some of my 'firsts,' in the order they happened. Take what you need!

HOW LONG WILL TRAINING TAKE? MY PLANNING VERSUS THE REALITY

I had far more lessons than I expected to need.

Here's my planning:

CBT: Pass in one day on a geared bike.

Ride my own 125 for six months. Decide whether I want to do DAS.

DAS: One day assessment on a 125 for Lesson 1.

Lesson 1 Full day on the 650

Lesson 2 Full day on the 650

Pass Mod 1

Pass Mod 2

This is what it actually was:

CBT: Passed on an automatic scooter by 2pm. Moved onto a geared 125 motorbike for another hour but didn't leave the car park. Didn't get above second gear.

A week later: One hour on the 125 in a car park, after that day's CBT students had gone home. Still struggling to change gears and nowhere near going on the road.

A week later: Another hour on the car park after the students had gone, getting worse. Confidence eroding. Dropped bike. Wanted to give up. Trainer forced me to go out onto the road or give up the idea altogether. Went out onto road, hit the kerb and landed up on the pavement. Decided to forget lessons and buy my own 125.

4000 miles later, begin DAS training for Mod 1 with a different school.

Day 1 Full day assessment on 125. Surprised to hear I am 'not ready' for the 650.

Day 2: Another full day on the 125, on road and slow-manoeuvring on a car park. Had ten minutes on the 650 at the end of the day, on the car park.

Practise like a demon between lessons.

Day 3: Morning on the 125. Stepped up onto the 650 for the afternoon. Rode 45 mins to the test site in Birmingham and did a couple of circuits (though not slalom or manual handling) I am not considered test-ready.

Day 4: Another full day on the 650. On road and in the car park in the morning, then back to the test centre in the afternoon. Still not considered test-ready: my slow control is hit and miss.

Six week wait for another lesson, owing to pandemic booking craziness.

Day 5: Same as Day 4. I have lost some skill on the bike during the six week wait. Drop bike on the car park attempting a U turn. Considered test-ready if I put in 'a lot' of work on my own.

I do a ton of work on my own.

Day 6: A week later. My test is still six days away, with no more lessons left. Training school fit me into their test site practice session to do a couple of circuits. I am all over the place and fail to complete a single U turn within the box.

Go home and spend one hour a day for the next five days on a car park doing U turns.

Day 7: Pass Mod 1

Day 8: Full day's Mod 2 training. Considered test-ready (good news, since the test is tomorrow morning)

Day 9: Pass Mod 2

The whole process cost me far more than I expected to pay, but I enjoyed all the DAS lessons (it was the only time I rode out with other people) and I felt, by the time I went in for my Mod 2, that I had been extremely well-trained. I felt I had been taught how to ride, not simply how to pass the test.

MY FIRST BIKE (JUNE 2020)

My first bike, Blanca, was a white Honda CB125F. I've mentioned her several times throughout the book: how big she seemed when she first arrived, how proud I was of her, how much I enjoyed having adventures on her.

She was more than a bike. She embodied freedom. She was physical proof of the personal journey I was making. I was working hard to build a stronger, braver version of myself, and I was reminded of this every time I climbed on her. She represented tenacity, determination, effort, resilience, excitement, possibilities. She expanded my world after Covid had crushed it down to nothing. Freed from the restrictions of the first lockdown, I was able to climb on her and escape. What a glorious feeling that was!

Looking back now, I made the right decision buying her. I needed time to build confidence and skill before starting DAS. I had learned on the same model and the familiarity helped.

But if I am being totally honest, I wish I had bought a 125 that pleased me aesthetically. The CB125F is a great bike but it was not 'me.' I like retro-looking bikes; the CBF is sleek and modern. Once I joined women's pages and saw what other women were riding, I did feel a little envious.

On the plus side, it made it easier to sell her. It must be *so* hard to sell a bike that has been your absolute pride and joy.

MY FIRST BIKER STOP (JULY 2020)

Biker stops can be a daunting as a learner. I remember the first time I pulled in to the main car park at Stow on the Wold one Sunday. Massed bikes with groups of men standing beside them, their heads turning to watch the new arrivals.

In truth, arriving wasn't the hardest part - leaving was. I clearly remember the nerves kicking in as I had to start Blanca and ride past them all to leave. *Don't stall*, I remember saying. *Don't stall*. It was very early days for me; stalling was something I still did, along with wobbling during slow manoeuvres.

But I did it fine - of course I did - and rode away feeling very pleased with myself. It was the highlight of my day.

If I had stalled - so what? All of those riders had stalled in the past - fact. They had all been beginners. I'm sure no one would have thought bad of me. And would it have mattered if they did? No.

MY MOD 1 (AUGUST 2021)

My examiner didn't specify a bay. I wanted to be sure I hadn't missed something, so I double-checked: 'Is there one in particular you want me to go in?'

He smiled. 'No. Either will do.'

If you are unsure, ask. Don't leave room for thoughts to creep into your head.

Manual Handling

There were two elements in the test that worried me, and this was the first. Acknowledging that, I made sure I took a deep breath before I began. I wheeled the bike slowly but surely, keeping my eyes firmly fixed where they needed to be. I also consciously dropped my left shoulder, which had proved a game-changer for me in training. I ran the mantra in my head: shoulder down, shoulder down.

I completed the manoeuvre remarkably easily. Once the bike was back on the stand, I shook my arms to release the tension. Took a breath. Believe me: you can do these things. The examiner won't think you are

a crazy

b time wasting

You won't be marked down for doing it. It is your time. Do what you need to do to get through. Which leads me very neatly to the next element -

Slalom and Figure of Eight

I wasn't worried about the riding side of this one, it was the direction that had foxed me in training. At least three times I had become confused about where I was supposed to be going. With this element, your choice of parking bay (for the manual handling) determines whether you will be doing your figure of eight clockwise or anti-clockwise. This had added to my confusion. It wasn't 'set.'

So knowing this, I was in no hurry to move off. I did this:

I climbed back on my bike.

I took a deep breath.

I looked at the cones and told myself where I would need to aim first.

I traced my finger in the air as I looked down the course. In and out of the cones, my finger traced the exact path I needed to take. I drew the figure of eight, then went round it again. Visualised the whole thing.

Satisfied that I knew what I was doing, I began.

After two figures of eight, I was amazed to see the examiner's hand go up, beckoning me over to the next element. I'm not kidding, when my examiner raised his hand to beckon me over for the next manoeuvre, the voice in my head went 'No way - I've got another four to do.'

I'm so glad I didn't say it out loud!

Slow control

The easiest element. Seriously, if you can't do this, you shouldn't be on the road. Since passing my Mod 2 and taking to the road as a Rider not a Learner, I have seen how utterly crucial it is.

U Turn

So. This was it. My possible undoing.

One of my instructors, Simon, had said to me *Do not begin until you are convinced you can do it*. I remembered that and was determined to take my time. So again, I sat on the bike and found a place of stillness. I reminded myself of the mantra I needed to use: *Shoulder, shoulder, shoulder, turn, look, aim*. I turned around to fix exactly what that 'look' referred to - an electricity pylon. Yes, it was still there. It hadn't disappeared since my last lesson, haha. I was good to go.

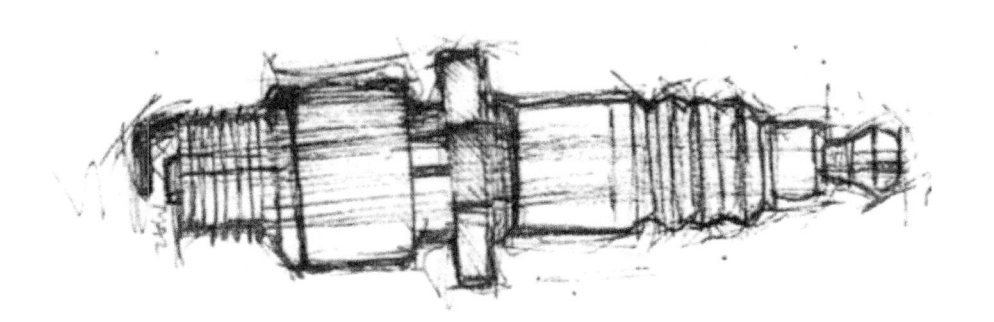

I took a deep breath. And it was at this moment that I allowed myself a rare negative command: *Do not fail this test because of three messy seconds*.

I had tried to reframe it to something positive, but nothing else carried the power of this. Because this was what it all came down to, wasn't it? I had trained and practised for weeks. Spent a small fortune on lessons but they had been worth it: I was physically capable of doing every element in this test.

But the Mod 1 allows no slack. That is why it is harder than the Mod 2. Hit a cone, go beyond a line, put a foot down for a single second - that's it. Fail.

Sitting there, about to begin the manoeuvre, it could all be over if I failed to turn hard enough and crossed the line.

How long does it take to do the turn? Two or three seconds. That's it. So that is what I had been telling myself the night before. You are going to bring your entire learning journey to a halt because of three messy seconds? Seriously?

I took another deep breath. Time was passing, but that was okay - I had plenty of it. The examiner seemed happy to wait.

I repeated Simon's question: Are you convinced you can do it?

Yes.

Shoulder, shoulder, shoulder, turn, look, aim.

I put the bike into gear and went.

And no word of a lie, I did it with a metre to spare. All those times I had crossed the line and here I was, pulling up miles clear. It wasn't perfect. I did a bit of a rev as I turned, but that was a fault, not a fail.

As I turned out, he didn't even give me a fault.

Controlled Stop

Isn't it funny how we can always find something to worry about? As I set off on the circuit to do my controlled stop, I thought: I'm nearly there. I'm fine with the fast elements. God, don't let me mess up one of the things I'm great at.

I ran all my mantras and did a perfect controlled stop. Stayed present and reminded myself I had to break the line of the U turn box as I turned, otherwise I would be marked for a second u-turn.

Emergency Stop

This is where I picked up my one and only fault. I reached the required speed and did a perfect stop, but there was a delay before I did it. 'For a moment, I didn't think you were going to do it,' the examiner told me later. 'I think you were looking down at the speedo when I raised my hand.'

I know why this happened. Just before going to the test centre, my instructor Mike had taken me onto a nearby housing estate to warm up my emergency stops and swerves. I wasn't happy about this. It felt wrong to me, using a residential street in that way. There could be cats or kids.

I did the manoeuvres but kept an eye on my speedo, and became aware that I was below the speed I would need to reach in the test. Clearly this stayed with me at an unconscious level - are you up to speed - causing me to look down, something I had never done in training.

Avoidance

I wasn't aware there had been a fault with my emergency stop. It felt fine to me. So as I went into this final element, I was thinking:

You have got this - don't mess up now.

This was another manoeuvre where I had to be absolutely clear where I as heading directionally. As I rode towards the bend I was telling myself over and over: *right, right, right.*

Round the bend.

Look for the cones.

Look at the inside, inside, INSIDE cone!

I flew through, perfectly.

I pulled to a stop and knew I had done it. Now I just had to concentrate for the final couple of minutes. Remember my shoulder checks. The test wasn't over till I was parked up and off the bike.

How did it feel to pass my Mod 1?

I was totally elated - and relieved. The harder test was behind me. I had this.

MY MOD 2 (SEPTEMBER 2021)

I was less relaxed on my MOD 2. I didn't *feel* nervous but my riding told a different story.

I think it was because MOD 1 felt like one more step along the path, whereas MOD 2 felt like a gateway. A kind of 'it can all end today and I will be free' way of thinking. I couldn't bear the thought of having to wait weeks for another test date. Then there was the money. I knew I would need another full day on the bike before any re-take, because I got rusty so fast.

Then my 125 broke down, three days before the test, and it became clear I had to get rid of it. I'd have no way of practising for a re-test…

Talk about piling the pressure on myself.

I set off feeling confident only to fumble at the very first junction. I stopped a bit clumsily and put my right foot down - something I never do. Instantly I felt I'd given the impression of being completely unbalanced on the bike, and we'd been riding for, what - less than two minutes?

As I rode on, I told myself 'He'll cut you some slack. You're still settling in. He knows people get nervous.'

But five minutes later, when he asked me to pull in behind a parked vehicle, I did another clunky one. Stopped in second gear. Definitely ragged.

Now the voice in my head told me to get a grip. Remembering I had an earpiece but no microphone, I took a few deep breaths and consciously made my body relax onto the seat.

We did the housing estate bit first then headed out into leafy lanes. Next came the dual carriageway and that was where I felt at home. Pushing the bike to seventy, I felt I was projecting confidence now, rather than nerves. Sometimes, on those urban roads, it feels like you're in a video game. There's so much coming at you, so fast. No sooner are you past the van driver opening the door when a woman crosses the road with a dog and a cyclist appears, fifty metres ahead.

On the fast roads, I felt some ease enter my body.

Back into the town centre and we were heading for one of the trickiest roundabouts: small, busy, perched on top of a hill, four exits and pedestrians everywhere, heading for the retail park next to it.

I saw a red car coming up the hill to my right. Made the decision to go and did it smoothly, but yikes, he seemed to be close behind me suddenly.

Was that it? An instant fail error? Had I caused another driver to slow down? No... had I?

Whatever, it was behind me. I could do nothing to change it. But as I rode on, I started to feel I was heading for a fail. So many moments that had been a bit woolly.

Then the examiner made a mistake. Oh, deep joy! You're not supposed to anticipate the route, because the examiner might have other ideas, but as we headed along the bypass, given the length of time we'd been out, I was expecting a 'take the next turning on the left' instruction. That would take us back towards the test centre. Except it didn't come. I slowed down a little, I couldn't help it. And finally his voice came: 'Oh, take the next slip road please. Sorry Cat, my mistake. I should have told you earlier.'

'He owes you one,' said the voice in my head. That made me smile.

Yes, we were heading back to the test centre, for sure. Two more roundabouts, straight ahead at both, and it would all be over.

'At the next roundabout turn left, please, turn left.'

What? No! See what I mean about anticipating the route?

So off we went, down another series of roads. And then calamity struck.

My training school had given me a brand-new bike that morning: a gorgeous Suzuki SV, showroom shiny, less than 100 km on the clock. One of their new fleet. This had thrown me to begin with. Yes, she was glorious, but I had never ridden her before. She was full height, and I had done most of my training on a lowered model. Really, was this a good idea on Test Day?

But I trusted my instructors and, within five minutes, I knew why they had given me this bike. She was a dream. So smooth... The gear changes! The throttle! She purred like a tiger. She had given me such a confidence boost.

But with five minutes left to go on the test, one of the mirrors came loose and swung towards me. Now I had no rear vision on my right. I pushed it back into place; a minute later it swung back.

What on earth should I do? If I had been with Laura, I would have told her I had a problem and needed to stop. But you have no microphone on an exam.

There was no way of stopping on the road I was now on. It was unfamiliar to me, but looked like a freeway. Should I turn off it? Should I just carry on? Or would he fail me for continuing on a bike that effectively had no mirror on the right?

I angrily pushed back the mirror yet again and cursed the school for giving me the bike. And with all this going on, there was no room in my brain to pay heed to the bike. My speed plummeted. I felt it go and I had made no gear change. I dropped down just in time, cursed again and carried on. By now I was totally convinced it was a fail.

A few minutes later, we rode into the compound where Laura was waiting with Dan, my training buddy from the previous day. Dan was going out next.

'How did it go?' he whispered. I frowned and gave a quick shake of my head. The examiner was opening his top box and pulling out a clip board. He hadn't said anything. I took this as a bad sign.

I flapped the mirror at Laura. 'This happened,' I said, testily. And yes, I was still simmering but also I did it loud enough for the examiner to hear. Maybe he didn't know why I'd had that crazy moment.

Sure enough, he came over. And bless him, he was such a lovely man, he started to ask Laura if it was okay. Could it be fixed before Dan's test? She said yes and duly fixed it. She didn't seem overly concerned.

And neither, as it turned out, was the examiner. I passed. I got four faults, two of them to do with moving off, so it could have been one of those early ragged ones.

But I was glad I made such a showy mention of the mirror, because he said to me 'I wondered why you suddenly slowed down like that.

It was very strange.'

Since I had passed, I confessed I hadn't known what to do. What should I have done?

'What would you have done if you were alone?' he said.

'Pulled over and fixed it.'

He nodded. 'That's what you could have done. Riding one-handed is never a good idea.'

But note this: he didn't fail me on it. Nor did he fail me for that red car on the roundabout, nor the ragged stops.

There's a saying I love:

When you're going through fire, keep going

That would be my Mod 2 advice. Whatever happens, put it behind you and keep going.

You do not need to be perfect, you simply need to be safe and smooth. What is important is the impression the examiner is getting. He said to me, 'I thought you were a very confident rider.' I was amazed at this, but thinking about it now, I did put on the gas when it was possible and I did cope with everything that came my way.

MY FIRST BIG BIKE (SEPTEMBER 2021)

My first big bike arrived today, two days after passing my Mod 2. I bought her online and she arrived in a van, all the way from Rotherham. What a stunner! I can't quite believe she is mine.

She is a sapphire blue Suzuki Gladius 650, the same bike I trained on. I have decided to call her Blue. Some people say: Don't buy the bike you trained on. Try as many as you can. There will be one that is more 'you.'

While I am sure that is true, Blue will suit me just fine. I want something I can continue to learn on, gain confidence on, begin touring on.

I wasn't sad to see my 125 being loaded onto the van as part of the deal. We have done six thousand miles together, but I have outgrown her. She will be someone else's joy soon. I have photos of her. That is enough.

Once the van had gone and I'd completed the final bits of admin - paying the road tax, telling the DVLA I no longer owned the 125 - it was time to go out on Blue. I could feel my heart beating as I put on my gear. Fear? Excitement? A bit of both. It takes courage to go out on a big bike on your own.

Not only had I dropped the instructor, I had lost the L plates. Other drivers would assume I was a seasoned rider - what difference would that make?

I headed out of town, aiming for the dual carriageway. A blast of speed always settles me: it makes me feel in control. I took the bike up to sixty and felt the exhilaration mounting. Two minutes later, I had reached the lorry up ahead and decided to go for an overtake. Up to seventy and I flew past, feeling joyously alive and free.

Next I turned off into the country lanes, and here I enjoyed the familiarity of a Gladius. I was pleased with my decision. I felt I had enough to worry about without having to get to grips with a totally new bike.

But that is me. Everyone is different. If I had been looking for a special bike, rather than a convenient one, maybe I would have taken my time choosing.

But it is September, with glorious weather forecast. I want to grab it. So at the time of writing, I am in a tea shop in Broadway, an impossibly sweet Cotswold town.

Blue purred up the main street, her blue and white bodywork gleaming. In my white jacket and helmet with pink flashes, I was unmistakably a girl, and I did notice a few men clocking us. I confess I felt super-sexy, which is not always your default state when you're nearing sixty!

I pulled into a parking bay, drew off my helmet, shook out my blonde curls like a shampoo advert. I know... Some of you might not approve of such behaviour. But I bloody loved it. I felt like I was having My Moment.

The only problem is, as I parked I went a bit too far into the bay. I tried to paddle back a metre, but the bay is cobbled. I won't be able to ride straight out - I'll have to do a bit of the dreaded manual handling in front of all the passers-by. That's where ego gets us!

MY FIRST MOTORWAY: THE M5 AT EXETER

My Devon road trip involved a four-lane stretch of the M5 at Exeter. I was excited about doing it. I learned in Redditch, which has a number of fast dual carriageways circling it, so I was confident I could join a motorway safely. But it was a still a high adrenaline, full-on ride. Totally exhilarating.

What do you need to ride motorways? I pondered this question five minutes after I had exited and was back on a quieter A road. This is how the experience seemed to me:

Confidence. You have to be confident you can handle it, especially if it's a busy stretch with exits at short intervals. There are vehicles on both sides of you and it is fast.

Speed. You need to be happy with bursts of acceleration because they are necessary. When you have to go across lanes, the safest way to do it is swiftly, decisively and assertively. You have to 'get on with it' as my instructor Laura would say. There is neither the time nor space to dither, looking anxiously over your shoulder while praying someone will let you across. You have to see where you need to go, find your space and move into it. And when everyone else is doing seventy, that means you will have to do it too.

Focus. It is full-on, without a doubt. Not only are you dealing with the road conditions and watching for what other drivers are doing, you are looking at the overhead gantries to see which lane you need to be in. You will need to give it your full attention.

I loved it! Given it was my first time, a quieter stretch would have been easier, for sure, but it's wonderful to step up to a challenge and handle it.

MY FIRST ROAD TRIP

I passed my Mod 2 in the morning and bought a bike in the afternoon. She arrived two days later. A week after that, I set off on my first road trip, to Devon. I went alone, taking in hills, severe bends, a car ferry and the aforementioned stretch of motorway at Exeter. It was fantastic. I did two hundred miles on the first day alone.

By Day Two, I was totally in awe of myself. I knew I had been extremely well-trained, and now it all came into play. I couldn't believe what I was handling. It was way beyond anything I had done in my DAS training.

South Devon is impossibly hilly. I was staying with friends in Brixham, which was a labyrinth of tiny streets with hairpin bends and astonishingly steep inclines, usually combined. Turning right at traffic lights on an extreme slope and the light is on red? Check.

In Mod 1 you do riding at walking pace, but not downhill! It is damned hard, especially when you're in a queue of traffic with no chance of overtaking because the road is too narrow.

Stopping at a junction when it's on a downhill slope is scary too. The whole weight of the bike seems to be behind you, pushing you towards the line. I couldn't remember doing one in the whole of my training, but they are commonplace in Devon.

That was one of the joys of the road trip though, facing all the challenges and handling them. Unfamiliar roads, physically unlike the ones you are used to. Busy tourist towns, with people wandering everywhere, paying no heed to the road. Following signs all the time, finding your way - I had no satnav.

You can't be thinking about the bike. You really have to be able to ride, because there isn't the headspace to deal with that alongside all the challenges.

One lesson I soon learned was this: Do not listen to your friend if they live local and do not ride a motorbike themselves!

My friend Cecilia is a sweetheart but she didn't understand how challenging the terrain was to a beginner. My left wrist was sore from all the clutch control I was having to do.

When I announced I was going out for a ride, she suggested I ride the coastal road. 'Go to Kingswear,' she said, 'and take the ferry across to Dartmouth.'

The road to the ferry was a winding, descending dead-end street packed with a snaking line of cars. As I reached the final bend, I saw a ferry man, beckoning me on - and I saw the ferry approach for the first time.

It was a concrete ramp with a 15% descent and it was wet. The metal ramp onto the ferry was wet too and MOVING, swaying from side to side with the swell. In that moment, I wanted nothing more than to turn back. I didn't want to tackle that descent. But it was impossible. I took a deep breath and went down, pulled up behind the parked car in front and felt my heart hammering.

The crossing was over in five minutes, and then I had the same at the other end, going up this time. When my turn came, I held back to let the cars in front clear the rise then went at it like Steve McQueen in The Great Escape. Whoosh! Right up. I rode on grinning from ear to ear. Well done me!

That night at supper, Cecilia's husband told me he knew a biker who had come off his bike on that same ramp. 'He was a courier, delivering some photos to my business,' he said. It was a squally day, the ramp was very wet and he skidded right off and ended up in the river, along with his bike. I don't know what Cecilia was thinking of, sending you down there. There's a much bigger ferry just five minutes further up the river!'

The thing I found most challenging about the trip was the parking. If you're used to parking a 125, it comes as a shock to pull over at the side of the road for a minute then find you can't lift the bike upright because you've parked on a camber. Twice I had to push the bike along the road until she was on flatter ground, cursing and grunting as I went.

Car parks were very tricky - so many of them weren't flat. It was impossible to ride onto Cecilia's drive: it was so steep I would never have been able to push Blue back up and out. So I had to descend backwards, inch by inch with my hand on the brake. Scary!

Once you're on a big bike, you must pay far more attention to where you are parking. If it doesn't feel easy, move on, specially if you are alone. Once the side stand is down and you're off the bike, it's too late. You're gonna be hauling and heaving like a sailor in a storm!

MY FIRST TUMBLE

My first 'off' was glamorous, as these things go. I was in Sardinia, riding one of those continental backroads that throw bends at you repeatedly, some of them hairpin. Up and down, the road seemed endless. The sky was clear blue, but it was December, early in the morning. My fingers were freezing inside my gloves. I wasn't feeling confident on the bike, a borrowed Yamaha Bolt 950 cruiser.

She looked and sounded glorious - sleek, curvaceous and with a distinctive cruiser cough. She turned heads wherever I went. Men would gather around her and sigh: *'Bella machina!'* But boy, she was heavy. At 250 kg, she was much heavier than I was used to.

Already I had failed even to even lift her upright when her owner Frank had casually parked her on a tiny incline. I had dropped her trying to manoeuvre in the drive. I had drifted terrifyingly (and potentially fatally) across the centre line on a right bend not once but *three* times.

Yes, she was fabulous when cruising along an open road, but on the twisties... *aargh*.

So it's fair to say I was struggling already when I hit the frosty patch. In my head, I was cursing the endless bends. It was not fun. When I saw the frost, I distinctly remember saying: 'Now *FROST*? Are you kidding me?!'

Maybe I panicked and maybe I used a bit of back brake - I don't know. I just remember the bike sliding away from under me. I fell to the left of her. Banged my head a little. Sat up but couldn't move my legs: both were pinned beneath the bike.

The road was very quiet, but a car arrived almost instantaneously from the other direction, coming round the bend. It stopped. A very handsome young Italian climbed out and sauntered towards me. I was gesturing: *lift it! Lift it!* I couldn't understand why he wasn't running. Frank had been riding ahead of me on his Triumph. He had clearly missed me and turned around. Now he arrived and the two of them lifted the bike off me.

'Medico?' said the Italian.

'No. No.' I was hurting but knew nothing was broken. My hip was hurting most. 'I'm okay.'

They pushed the bike to a lay-by. Conveniently, I had come off right next to one. Frank gave me a hug, satisfied himself I was okay, then turned his attention to the bike. I had broken the gear lever; she was unrideable.

We rode back to base (nearly two hours away) on Frank's bike, fetched his jeep and trailer, returned to the Bolt, loaded her on and that was that. Road trip over on Day Two.

So how did it feel to go down?

It was fast but also a bit slow motion. I was aware I was going down but there was nothing I could do about it.

It hurt, but my bruises weren't spectacular and caused me no discomfort. Most were caused by the bike, not by hitting the tarmac. The armouring worked. I had no hip armour in my trousers, hence the bruise. Though to be fair I was going very slow. Under thirty, for sure.

MY FIRST EUROPEAN ROAD TRIP

I didn't believe we would get as far as Sardinia, to be honest. That was the plan: to meet in Calais, ride down through France via the Loire valley to Biarritz. Head along the northern edge of the Pyrenees, with a detour down to the principality of Andorra on the way. Along the coast of southern France, Marseilles to Nice. Through Monaco and on into Italy. Catch the ferry from Livorno to Sardinia.

But I reckoned it would soon become apparent to my riding buddy Frank that my cornering was so unreliable, I wouldn't be safe riding *anywhere* with hills, let alone mountains. Our trip was supposed to be a month, but I honestly felt we might spend a week riding around lowland France and then Frank, bored beyond belief, would call it a day and head for the hills without me.

That didn't happen.

What *did* happen was I rode 3213 miles, to Sardinia and back. I rode two mountain passes in the Pyrenees and one in the Italian Alps. I rode serpentine coastal roads in Spain and Sardinia. I rode through a string of impossibly busy city centres, including Barcelona, plus dozens of towns and hundreds of villages. I handled ramps in car ferries and underground car parks. I rode on grass, gravel, sand. Coped with wind so scary, it reduced me to tears. I rode in 42 degree heat. I rode at 100 mph on the motorways. I did more than a hundred fast and furious road tunnels at Genoa. I did ascents and descents, and stayed on Sardinian roads that never stopped bending. I did up/down hairpins, both on country roads and, shockingly, right in the centre of busy towns.

I generally did hairpins very badly. Sometimes unsafely. Always excruciatingly slowly. I dragged the back brake mercilessly on far too many bends. I was over-cautious and under-confident. I hated long, winding descents with a passion and still don't see why anyone would choose a twisty road over a straight one.

But hey, I did it. And I firmly believe it is better doing something badly than not doing it at all, as long as you live to tell the tale.

Riding Highlights

To be clear, this wasn't a biking trip. It was a road trip by bike. I was far more interested in seeing medieval architecture than riding 'biker' roads, and I didn't want to be constantly stressed out, riding above my skill level. So our routes were chosen accordingly. Frank was often bored witless by long stretches of A road, but as a newbie, I loved the bigger roads - I was able to relax and see the view instead of having to concentrate like a demon.

So, six riding highlights, in the order they came…

1. **The M25.**

Sounds crazy, I know, but I love a busy motorway. That is when I feel most alive on a bike. I love the awareness, the flow of information, the assessing and reacting. The sudden bursts of speed, the lane changing, the decision making, the feeling of being in flow. I love filtering. So the M25 was a joy for me, I had never ridden it before.

2. **The French & Italian Motorways**

Loved them! So fast and so disciplined. No one cruises in the middle lane. You pull out, overtake, return to your lane.

In Italy, the drivers took no prisoners. The outside lane often had a line of fast cars cruising along but they seemed unhappy for a bike to join them. I found I was hassled a lot less if I indicated an intention to return to my lane once I had overtaken.

3. **Riding through avenues of plane trees**

Napoleon planted many of the avenues, to provide shade for marching troops. I never lost my delight at entering these gorgeous green tunnels.

4. **Riding through miles of sunflower fields**

Glorious. How can anyone's spirit not be raised at such a sight?

5. **Coastal roads**

We did the fabulous coastal road at Cinque Terre, a UNESCO status landscape where villages cling to rocky mountaintops set against the shimmering backdrop of the Ligurian Sea. We began at La Spezia and headed north towards Genoa. Highly recommended.

In Sardinia, one of the very best roads is the coastal road from Alghero to Bosa. Stunningly beautiful. From Bosa, we rode back across the mountains in the direction of Tempio Pausina and had the roads totally to ourselves.

Sardinian roads are *very* bendy. A hundred bends in a row is not unusual, and they are sharp ones, not long, sweeping ones. The island is also mountainous and craggy, with majestic coastal views.

A friend of mine used to road race for Ducati, and he told me he had raced for them on Sardinia. The iconic biker route is the SS125, also known as the *Orientale Sarda*, which is on the east coast. We didn't have time to do it this year, but I have done it by Jeep in the past. It's a fabulous road, full of bikers, with a legendary biker cafe (Bar Silana) located near the start of the famous Gorropu gorge hike. Gorropu is one of the deepest gorges in Europe.

If you want bends and beaches, Sardinia has to be on your list. We took the ferry from Barcelona to Porto Torres and returned from Olbia to Livorno. (Grimaldi Lines) It wasn't expensive.

6. **Mont Cenis Pass, Italian Alps (SS25/D1006 north of Susa)**

This glorious road takes you from Italy (west of Turin) into France, via alpine peaks and past a dazzling turquoise blue lake. At its highest point, the road is 2800m. You also ride though ski resorts and past an astonishing clifftop citadel. Riding it was one of the best days of my life.

There were plenty of bikers using it, and it's well served with cafes at various points. It's not especially challenging for an experienced rider, just hugely enjoyable I guess. But it was perfect for me, and I was so glad Frank found it.

It's difficult being a beginner on alpine roads. You can't learn unless you practise, but you are acutely aware how slow you are. Holding traffic up is stressful, and it's upsetting when drivers beep you. It erodes your confidence. You're trying your best, for goodness' sake.

This road, though full of bends and hairpins, has plenty of long, wide stretches for people to pass. The descent was long, for me at least. Thirty minutes? More? I was exhausted by the time I had done it. But it would have been such a shame to have ridden through the Alps on the main A road. This route was a little daunting, but anything is possible, one bend at a time.

Riding Lowlights

We learn more from the hard parts than the easy, it's true, but it doesn't stop them being deeply unpleasant at the time. Here are a few of the lows.

1. **The Pyrenees Descent, from Frontera del Portalet to Laruns**

Looking at it now, on Google maps, it doesn't look too bad. I definitely tackled worse, later in the trip, with less fuss.

But it had been a long day, I was tired and my hands were cramping. We had just made a short stop at the Spain/France border, where I had asked Frank how far it was to our accommodation. He said 30km. So in my head, I was thinking "Great. Nearly there.'

What I didn't know was those 30km were all downhill. It was one long, torturous descent of never-ending bends, with a few hairpins thrown in for good measure. Very few long stretches where drivers could get past. It was a nightmare. I felt completely trapped. There was no turn off. I could only keep going as the cars queued behind me.

And they did queue. As my confidence and energy drained, my speed dropped even lower. I was crawling round simple corners, terrified they would turn out to be hairpins. 30 mph, 25 mph… The descent took me forty-five minutes. I was emotionally shredded by the end of it.

The worst point came midway through, when I managed to pull over to let a long queue past. I didn't stop, simply put on my indicator, dropped my speed even lower and gestured for them to pass. Except one campervan didn't pass. It stayed behind me, going as slowly as I was. So slowly, I looked over my shoulder to see what the hell was wrong. I found the driver roaring with laughter and the passenger filming me with his phone. So I was going to be on TikTok now, was I? The stupid British woman and her pathetic attempts to handle a twisty road.

I angrily waved at them to go, go. They did, beeping me as they went. I still had another ten km or so to go. Sometimes you just have to dig deep.

Incidentally, it was only many days later that I realised Frank was seeing the shape of the bends on his satnav. Whereas I, the one who really needed the help, was effectively driving blind. And with no comms, he couldn't give me any advance warning. Little wonder I was so stressed.

2. **The Savage Wind on the Motorway from Narbonne**

I am used to riding in wind. My part of Warwickshire seems excessively windy most of the time. But the wind on this particular stretch of motorway was in another league.

The wind socks by the side of the carriageway were horizontal. Every bridge had a sign warning caravanners to slow down. My bike Blue felt like she was going to slide from under me. I was having to counter-steer simply to stay upright.

But still there were lorries we had to overtake. Frank was leading. Whenever he pulled out, I had to brace myself to follow. The punch of wind as I passed each lorry was terrifying. Once I was blown completely into the next lane.

On and on and on it went, for mile after mile. No mention of a turn off or a service station. I had that feeling again, the one I get on too-long descents, the feeling of being trapped. Held in some private hell I cannot escape. All I could think of was how profoundly unpleasant it was to be there, on a bike, in such conditions. I was shouting inside my helmet: I just want this to be *OVER*.'

Finally there came a chance to pull in at a rest stop. I climbed off the bike, my hands shaking with the adrenaline, and started to cry. It was all too much. Too scary, too hard, too relentless, too everything.

Frank was amazed at how upset I was.

'You're riding fine,' he said. 'I can see you in my mirror. If you were struggling, I would see it. But you're not. You're handling it. And it isn't that windy anyway.'

'*Are you kidding me?* The wind is *savage*.'

He shook his head. 'It's not. Look at the trees.'

They were barely moving. It was the weirdest thing, and I experienced it later in the trip too: a wind-tunnel of a road with still trees lining it.

'It's the heat,' he said. 'The cooler wind from the sea hitting the hot air over the land - it makes things feel turbulent. But mostly it is in your head.'

We had to carry on, another 30km or so. Though curiously, once I was back on the motorway I was fine. I accepted I couldn't change the wind or the thermal buffeting, I could only change my attitude towards them. So instead of battling to hold on, I loosened my grip and let my bike dance in the wind like a feather.

I was never bothered by wind again.

3. **Riding in the Wrong Clothes**

The first thing you notice when you ride on the continent is that no one wears protective gear when it's hot. Shorts and tee shirts are the norm. On the coast, I saw girls riding pillion in little more than bikinis. The only exception is the guys on racing bikes heading into the hills. They wear leathers. But everyone else - no.

Frank did the entire trip in shorts and a tee shirt, putting on a jacket or trousers only when it was getting cold. No boots or gloves. Whereas I had the full kit on at all times: mesh jacket, mesh trousers, gloves and boots. Even in 42 degree heat.

I had to. Last time I rode in Italy, I came off a bike on a mountain road. There was every possibility I would do it again. I was also far more vulnerable at junctions than Frank - my attention was always focussed on following him, rather than the movements of drivers. With no comms, my signalling and road positioning was erratic at times.

So I was resigned to wearing the gear, but I always hated it, especially when we stopped for a 'quick' coffee that unexpectedly became a thirty-minute walk around a town. I carried a skirt and flip flops in my top box for proper breaks, and would always get changed, despite the time it took to pack everything away. But these spontaneous longer breaks were always difficult, with me sweltering in trousers and boots while everyone around me was cool in cotton and sandals.

Being cold was even worse. I left the UK in the middle of a heatwave and, having previously been to Italy in July, my thoughts when packing had focussed almost entirely on keeping cool and keeping the weight down. So I had packed one long-sleeved vest but that was about it. It never occurred to me that it would rain, so I had no waterproofs.

But a week into the trip, the weather in France turned for a few days, and my mesh clothing was next to useless. I was cold to the bone for hours on end. Holding on, longing with all my heart to be in a car.

I longed to be in a car on very hot days too, to be honest, wearing a scrap of a dress and flip flops. In extreme heat, there is no joy in being on a bike in full gear. The wind does not blow through your hair; the sun does not kiss your skin. I lumbered into every pit stop like a fevered rhino. In towns, I gazed enviously at girls who skipped out of cafes in strappy dresses and sandals, slipped on a helmet and rode away on their scooters.

I bet they didn't get heat rash on their bum cheeks.

INTERVIEW WITH LAURA SMITH

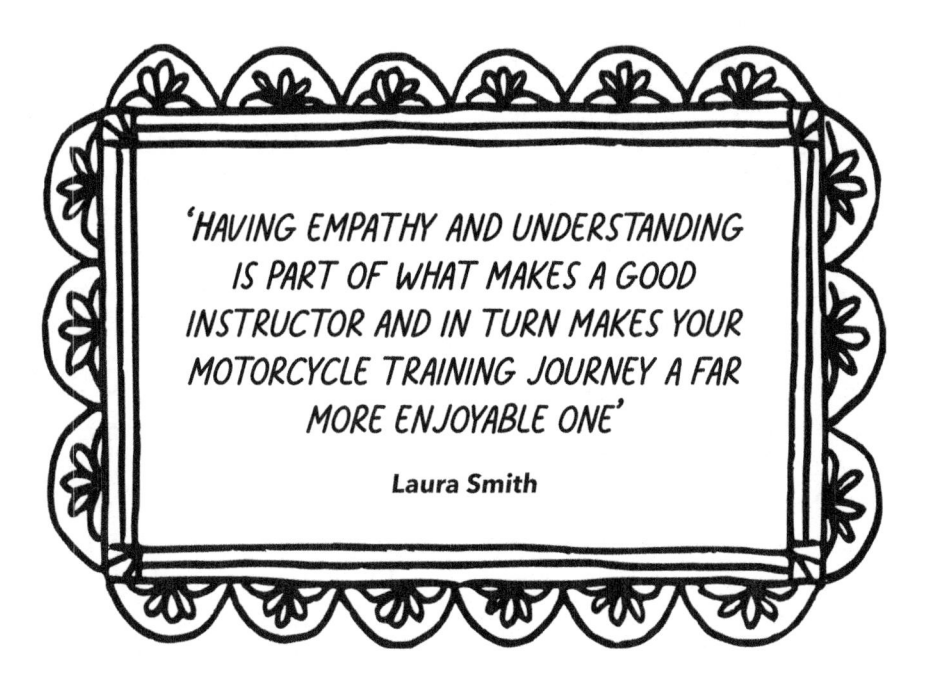

> 'HAVING EMPATHY AND UNDERSTANDING IS PART OF WHAT MAKES A GOOD INSTRUCTOR AND IN TURN MAKES YOUR MOTORCYCLE TRAINING JOURNEY A FAR MORE ENJOYABLE ONE'
>
> **Laura Smith**

Laura was my main trainer when I did DAS and I continue to do advanced training with her. She is a wonderful instructor and women travel from across the UK to train with her.

I thought it would be great to hear her thoughts on some of the issues raised in this book. So if you'd like to hear what she has to say on choosing a training school, riding a 125 or the challenges of being a short rider, read on…

What would be your advice for a complete beginner?

Ride a bicycle first. I remember when I did my CBT, that was one of the first things the instructor asked me: Can you ride a bicycle? And I was like, 'Of *course* I can!' but it was probably ten years since I'd been on a bicycle. Luckily for me, I had quite good balance. Perhaps it was because I'd done dancing as a kid, and gymnastics and stuff like that. But for most people, you can't teach balance in a CBT. It has to be something you've already got.

Where people trip up is the second exercise, which is slow control. Figure of eights and u-turns within the first hour of riding! If you're not used to riding on two wheels, then you're going to struggle, because you've got enough to think about with clutch and throttle and back brake, trying to guide the bike where you want it to go, trying to relax as much as possible. Whereas if you've ridden a push bike before, you've already got that experience and you feel more comfortable turning the bars and getting the bike leaning over without feeling you're going to drop it.

Do your research is what I'd say next, so you get the right school for you, the right trainer. There are lots of training schools out there, and some of them are more likely to have a predominantly male customer base. So when you come through as a female, and you might be shorter than average or you might be feeling really anxious, and the guys that they get through *aren't* generally like that, then the trainers might not have the right tone, the right attitude towards you, to get the best out of you. I would have *loved* a female trainer, but I couldn't find one when I was learning.

The reason I get so many females coming to me from around the country is because they've had a really bad experience at their local school, and then they say, 'D'you know what? I can't risk it... I can't risk going to another instructor who might treat me like that. I need to find someone who might understand me.'

And thirdly I'd say *don't feel pressured*. A lot of females come in because their partners or mates are trying to get them to do it, and actually, learning to ride a motorcycle is really difficult. If your heart isn't 100% in it, you're really not going to be able to achieve it easily, because it is something that you've got to really want. Especially on training days when it's chucking it down with rain and you're cold and you're wet and the instructor isn't allowing you to move on because you can't get the figure of eight right. When the pressure's on, you've got to *really* want it.

After CBT, do you advise buying a 125?

I think if you're going to ride on a 125, ultimately it should just be a stepping stone to doing your motorcycle test. When you move onto DAS, having your own bike can be really beneficial. You can practise all the skills you learn in your lessons. So for some people, having a 125 for a short time is ideal.

But I certainly wouldn't get in the trap of riding out with people on bigger bikes, because that always leads to more problems. When I have students who have done their CBT and they're coming back to do their DAS, a lot of the time I have to try to slow them down, because they are a bit frantic about trying to keep up, and the only place on a low-powered machine you can really keep up is when you come into junctions and roundabouts. So they're not slowing down enough, and they're actually a little bit dangerous sometimes, coming into the hazards too quickly. I have to unpick all those bad habits they've picked up.

When you are under instruction, everything is kept contained, so you are never out of your ability because the instructor dictates that. Whereas when you're out with others, with people who can ride quicker than you or have more experience than you, there's always that risk that you'll follow them. And you can't do what they can do, because your skill level is less because you've been riding for less time and you've got less knowledge. It's just a bit of a recipe for disaster.

I'm not against people getting on a 125 to help them improve if that is what they need to do, and some people *do* need to do that to build confidence. But this is where partners and friends who are bikers already can be a bit of a double-edged sword. I know they can be really encouraging and want you to get your full licence, which is great. But they shouldn't pressure you to go quicker.

I suppose it can be frustrating if you're on a bigger bike and you're riding with somebody who can't get up to speed. But at the end of the day, they know what size bike you're riding, and if they have ever been in that situation, they should understand how it feels. But I think that is where some guys are not so good, on the whole empathy thing. They forget or they find it hard to put themselves in that situation.

What are the specific problems that women face?

People get upset on social media about men and women having different traits when it comes to learning, but I have to be honest: there are. It is a generalisation but guys generally give it a go and have more confidence to start with. Whether they feel anxious or not, they wouldn't show it, whereas women would. Women say, 'I'm doing something I've never done before and I'm not sure how it's going to go.'

So I think women tend to hold themselves back a tiny bit more than the guys do. I think they are scared of making mistakes because they want to do it right, and that holds them back a bit.

Where they *are* different to the guys is they are usually fantastic listeners! When you give women an instruction, they just get on and do it, whereas with the guys, it takes them three or four goes before they take on board what you're trying to say. Sometimes they even have to make few mistakes first before they decide they should probably listen to what the instructor is saying as it's beneficial!

Women are usually much tidier-skilled riders than the guys, who can be quite sloppy if you like. The girls do everything in order and that makes for a much tidier rider as a result. Women are there to learn. They don't necessarily have the attitude that they already know how to do it. They come as novice riders and they listen to what I have to say and try to apply it. It might take them longer initially to get riding on the whole, but once they've got it, there's no stopping them! So usually they take longer at CBT level, then once they've got it, they're just fantastic.

We had a female student recently and it took her a *really* long time to get to her onto the 650, mainly because she was so busy. She'd got so many other ties; she had kids, she was working full time, studying full time and she was trying to fit in her training around all of that. But the other big problem she had was that she was only 4'11" with size 3 feet! So even getting on a Gladius was a really scary situation to be in, and her skill level had to be ten times better than any of the other riders at the school, because one tiny little mistake might mean the bike falling over.

If you are a guy and you're 5'11", you might make a mistake, but you can sometimes rectify it, because your ability to stand the bike up and stop it falling over is better. Whereas for her, she had to really be 10/10 to get on the 650. And she nailed both her Mod 1 and Mod 2 with clean sheets, because her standard was just *so* much better than the guys. But she had to work a lot harder for it. Even though we've got a lowered bike, it's still nearly 200kg to push and shove around on the Mod 1. It's a big old heavy lump to try and manoeuvre if you're not used to that.

Different body shapes can definitely have an impact. If you're small, gear changing is harder. The biting point on the clutch for example... You can adjust the clutch on a lot of bikes so the biting point is closer, but the actual lever is still quite a long way out. So you've still got to pull that clutch in, which can affect your steering. U-turns... If you've got really short arms, you might struggle to get a good u-turn done unless you get the right coaching and feel confident.

Curvier riders, riders with big boobs, maybe a tummy... This can make a difference if you are trying to lean forward, trying to steer the bike. Guys don't have that issue necessarily. When I ride my ZZR14 I've got a huge tank bag on the front of it which is great for touring, but my boobs really do get in the way!

So there are subtle differences that perhaps we don't talk about. If you are shorter, it is going to be harder unfortunately, until they start making bikes that are more suitable for shorter riders. You haven't got the same amount of arm length, the same ease with the clutch, the same ease with the brakes and just generally it's more difficult.

At the other end of the spectrum, some of the guys who are 6'4" and trying to ride a 125, with their massive feet applying the brakes... That's not easy either! But I would say it's easier if you are a bit bigger than a bit smaller.

It never really occurred to me until I had to ride a GS a friend had bought. I had gone to collect it with him, and he said 'You can ride it back.'

I was literally on the tips of my bike boots when I lifted the bike up. And at that point I thought 'That's okay, I just won't put my feet down until I get back to his house.'

And as an accomplished rider, I am confident to be able to do that. I'll just approach every junction and roundabout without stopping, and I know I can do that. But not everybody can do that, especially when they first start. And it was that moment when I was like 'Oh my God, if I was 5'2 and getting on a motorbike for the first time, this is very scary.' And I don't think many people understand that.

Do men get anxious too?

Oh yes. I think some more than others. I think perhaps unfortunately men are encouraged not to show it quite so much, but I can see it. As an instructor you learn to pick up on the vibes, you can see where they're struggling. If their knees or legs or arms are shaking, you can see all those things. I just think women are far better at verbalising how they feel.

I did a Yamaha Off-Road Experience last year for Women Only Motorcycle Training, and the guy in charge said, 'We're going to split you into two groups now. We're going to have a group of more confident riders and a group of less confident riders. Who is going to go in the confident group?'

And everybody just sat on their bikes in silence! In the end, one of the ladies said 'Can we rephrase that and have 'the people who are really shitting it' and 'the people who aren't shitting it quite so much?'

Because none of them felt confident.

What a completely different attitude that was to when I did the same course with a mixed group. The guys who perhaps aren't always that good happily put themselves in the 'top' group, the A group. It was astonishing really.

How to be more confident

The more skill you can get on a bike, the more confident you will become. There are things that you might not be taught by your instructor. Little nuggets of information that will help.

I'm all for people being more confident by having a positive mindset, but as a not-naturally confident person, I have found my confidence through being more skilled on the bike in the first place. I feel more confident because I understand what I am doing on the motorbike and what controls are going to affect it and how. I think a lot of people don't understand that, especially at CBT level. We don't go into the detail: what happens when you apply the front brake in a corner , what happens when you apply the rear brake in a corner, what happens when you put the power on in a corner, or what happens when you put the power on as you exit at a junction. How can you control that?

The more tools you have in your tool box, the more confident you will become. It's like when you start a new job and you feel like you know nothing, but it's the experience that gives you confidence. You learn on the job. But I would never recommend learning to ride a motorcycle through just experience, because you can become really good at being bad, because you've learned all the wrong skills.

Motorcycling is a never-ending journey. You never finish learning!

Women Only
MOTORCYCLE TRAINING

Women Only Motorcycle Training is specifically designed for those who want to learn to ride, without added pressure or judgment in a pro-woman environment.

Laura Smith, Motorcycle Instructor and owner of Women Only Motorcycle Training has a passion for skill and technique, ensuring riders feel confident in their own ability.

'The key is to not rush the basics. Giving students the knowledge, skills and more importantly the time to improve without feeling rushed or that they're not good enough is imperative. This is the key to confidence and in keeping more women riding.'

- Offering an exclusive 2-and-a-half-day CBT (with RMT Motorcycle Training)
- Direct Access Scheme training (pay as you go)
- Mod 1 & Mod 2
- Enhanced Rider Scheme training
- Advanced

Interested in training with Laura? Google "Women Only Motorcycle Training" or type in the URL below. Want to chat with Laura? Drop her an email and she will arrange a good time to give you a call.

WOMT.co.uk info@womt.co.uk

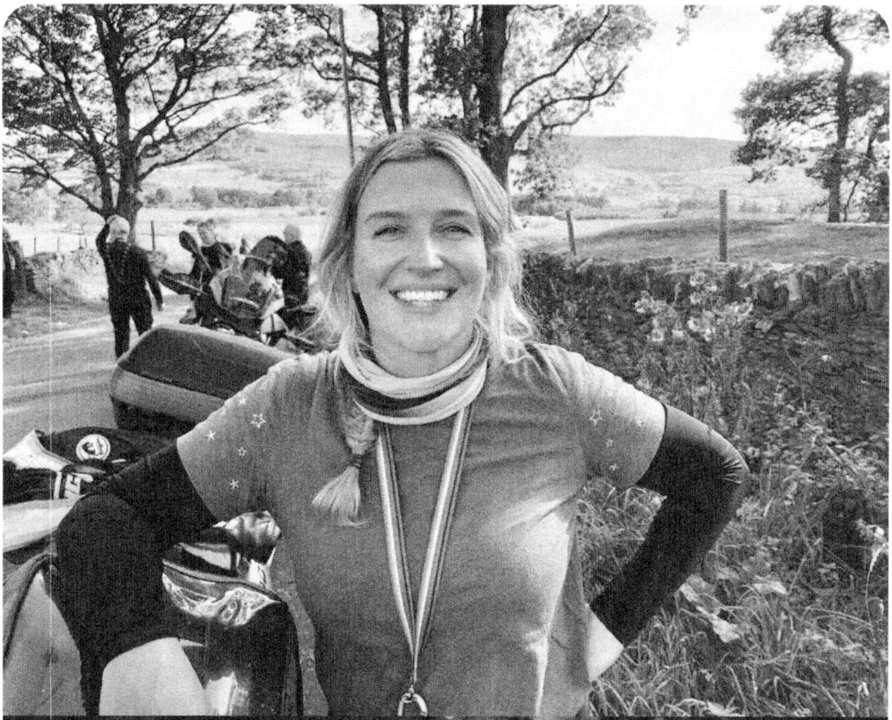

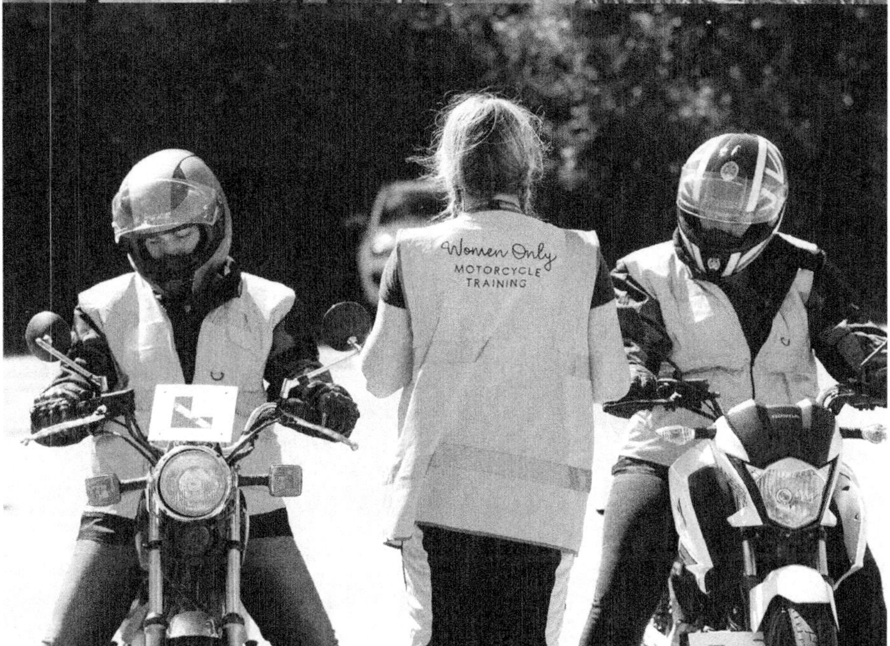
Women Only
MOTORCYCLE
TRAINING

Hi! I'm MazArty, Angela Holbrook, from Staffordshire UK.

I've always got many hobbies on the go - crochet, macrame, knitting, painting stones, gardening, motorcycling. I play ukelele and sing in a punk band! But I have to say, art is my main go-to.

I am a self-taught artist and I've drawn, as far as I can remember, from a young age. I like to work in many different mediums ie pastels, acrylics, graphite, coloured pencils, but mainly watercolour & pen, specialising in motorcycle, pet and animal portraits.

I started drawing motorcycles when I started riding motorbikes, twenty-odd years ago.

I take on many commissions throughout the year, and I work at many craft shows and biker events, selling my greetings cards, original art, prints and now I have a tee shirt range which is becoming very popular.

You can see most of my work on Facebook and Instagram pages

- MazArty.

MAZARTY

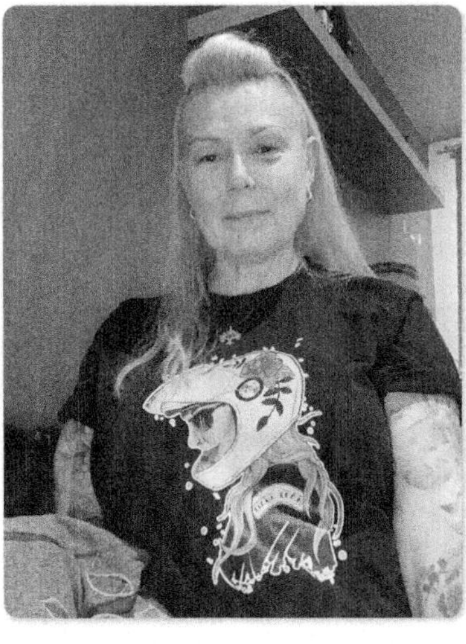

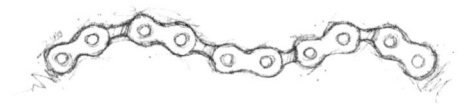

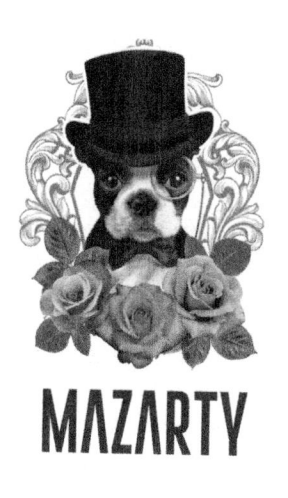

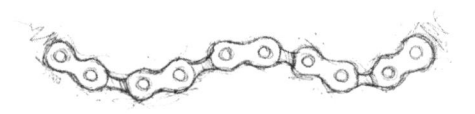

Hi! I'm Cat.

I began riding motorcycles at the age of fifty-eight. Being a late starter, I have thrown myself into road tripping! Within a year of passing my full licence, I rode my Suzuki Gladius 'Blue' to Italy and back, via the Pyrenees and the Italian Alps. My most recent adventure was a 4000km road trip around Thailand from the islands of the eastern seaboard to the mountains of the north. Now I'm planning a trip to Ireland to ride the Wild Atlantic Way. But mostly I ride in the Cotswolds, which I love.

I also love the scent of jasmine, reading books and drinking tea. I love to feel my heart beating faster. I get very excited at airports. I work hard to be lucky, laugh a lot and will eat toast even if it falls on the floor.

My favourite quote is by Charles Bukowski:

'The gods will offer you chances. Know them. Take them.'

Cat is a performance storyteller, appearing at festivals and theatres internationally, on BBC radio and in schools.
She is also a best-selling author.

catweatherill.co.uk

Find me on Facebook
@Motorcycle Confidence For Women
for extra tips, videos and encouragement

If you have found this book helpful, please leave a review on Amazon.

HAPPY RIDING!

Cat x

Printed in Great Britain
by Amazon